- **Negotiating contracts and agreements**

- **Understanding culture and customs**

- **Marketing products and services**

An American's Guide to Doing Business in

India

A Practical Guide to Achieving Success in the Indian Market

Eugene M. Makar

BUSINESS
Avon, Massachusetts

D0288350

To the 800 million Indians living on less than $2 a day

Published by
Adams Business, an F+W Publications Company
57 Littlefield Street, Avon, MA 02322. U.S.A.
www.adamsmedia.com

ISBN 10: 1-59869-211-9
ISBN 13: 978-1-59869-211-2

Printed in Canada
J I H G F E D C B A

Library of Congress Cataloging-in-Publication Data
Makar, Eugene M.
An American's guide to doing business in India /
Eugene M. Makar.
p.   cm.
ISBN-13: 978-1-59869-211-2 (pbk.)
ISBN-10: 1-59869-211-9 (pbk.)
1. International business enterprises—India. 2. Investments,
Foreign—India. 3. Joint ventures—India. 4. India—Commerce—
United States. 5. United States—Commerce—India.
I. Title. HD2899.M345 2007
330.954—dc22   2007015782

This publication is designed to provide accurate and authoritative information
with regard to the subject matter covered. It is sold with the understanding
that the publisher is not engaged in rendering legal, accounting, or other
professional advice. If legal advice or other expert assistance is required, the
services of a competent professional person should be sought.
—From a *Declaration of Principles* jointly adopted by a Committee of the
American Bar Association and a Committee of Publishers and Associations

Many of the designations used by manufacturers and sellers to distinguish
their product are claimed as trademarks. Where those designations appear
in this book and Adams Media was aware of a trademark claim, the designations have been printed with initial capital letters.

This book is available at quantity discounts for bulk purchases.
For information, please call 1-800-289-0963.

CONTENTS

ACKNOWLEDGMENTS

Let me first acknowledge you, the reader of this book. I believe India affords many opportunities to those brave enough to take the chance and astute enough to take advantage. Success in India vis-à-vis the United States or Europe, however, requires vastly different skills, enormous patience, careful planning, and perpetual flexibility.

India is an ancient land that is just beginning to emerge from a very long slumber. It is a country undergoing tremendous change—if that is all you take away from this, then you are already ahead in the game.

This book is written for Americans by an American. I have pulled few punches and attempted to depict the business landscape as realistically as I see it. I sincerely hope that this helps you to climb your own Everest, as Indians are fond of saying. I know that it has helped me climb mine.

I want to express my sincerest gratitude to my good friend and associate, Tulsi Tawari, whose inspiration touched me from halfway around the world. I am very happy for him that his homeland is finally on a path that can benefit all of her people. I also want to give my sincerest thanks to Larry Tuller, who patiently helped me peel back many of life's layers during the development of this book.

Part I

Introduction to India

If you're reading this book, it means you're curious about business in India. That's good because it also means you're thinking critically about a venture that could be different from any other international investment you've ever made. You realize that you're likely to be unprepared for many of the things you'll be encountering and experiencing. The first part of this book provides the information and thought-triggers that can and will make or break your plans. I cannot emphasize this strongly enough. You may only get one chance at a business situation in India—and complete preparation and awareness are going to be crucial to its success.

The first step in that preparation is to develop a solid understanding and awareness of the country and its people. Without these, you're putting the rudder of your ship in someone else's hands, if not tossing it overboard—is that really what you want to do?

The India we read about and see on television and the Internet is just one tiny slice of a country with a remarkably non-Western past. Modern India is largely a veneer of recent creation over a culture with very ancient roots that burrow back thousands of years. Respecting and understanding India's social and business cultures are the important keys to unlocking your success. The best way to do this is to view India as the product of its history and to see that some of its components are unique: more than twenty official languages set many internal state and cultural borders; three major religions, and a half dozen more minor religions, formed international boundaries and foment ongoing social and political unrest; a philosophically based culture defines and perpetuates inertia, stability, and bias for more than one billion people; free-for-all business systems hatched out during decades of backward-looking, post-independence corruption; and a young population anxiously and eagerly searching for its future.

Chapter 1

India in the Twenty-First Century

Every day another article, newsflash, television report, or blog about India appears in the media. Some of these are insightful, others are useful, a few are misleading, but most offer only a peek into a world that is truly foreign to most Americans. India is a land of enormous opportunities. Plan your strategy well, and you will be able to share in the miracle. Rush in hastily, and you are likely to miss out, or worse. India also is a land of enormous differences. It is rapidly changing and yet staying the same—a land of contrasts that can keep you baffled. I am not the first person to say this, nor will I be the last. Here are some facts to get started:

- An Indian is near the top of the *Forbes* list of the world's billionaires, and six of the top 125 on the list are Indians, yet 800 million of their countrymen live on less than $2 a day.
- Much of Indian culture is rooted in events reaching back as far as 3,500 years, yet the country's modernization is being driven by half a billion people under the age of twenty-five.
- India has nuclear power and the atomic bomb, yet residents suffer from HIV/AIDS at a rate second only to the Republic of South Africa.

Over $25 million U.S. dollars flow into India every day. A Reuters survey placed India at the top of the heap for long-term strategic investment due to the nation's continued efforts to reform its economic systems. A.T. Kearney has India second on its list of most attractive countries for foreign investment. Speaking about foreign-company operations in India, the Federation of Indian Chambers of Commerce and Industry (FICCI) points out the following:

- 70 percent are making profits.
- 84 percent are planning expansions.
- 91 percent foresee opportunities in sectors other than their own.

High-profile Indians all around the world publish articles and newsletters encouraging social and political reforms on the home front so that the benefits of the country's emergence diffuse down to all the people. Seemingly unafraid to step on anyone's toes, the Central Government repeatedly commits resources and rupees to policies and practices intended to jump-start change. The wheels are in motion and India is headed in the right direction.

Can she sustain her momentum? I believe so, provided the government continues to exercise proper management and all levels and sectors in the economy are fully committed to stay the course and tighten their belts, if necessary. The biggest and most critical tasks before India's Union Government (also called the Central Government or Government of India) is effecting the country's change from a mostly agrarian economy to a balanced economy with a significant job-producing manufacturing sector. To be successful, this must be sustainably done without leaving millions of people behind and the environment in ruins. The consequences of failure would be felt throughout the world.

I believe that the best long-term opportunities for most American businesses in India are in manufacturing for export. This is the sector where India is putting the most muscle. It takes advantage of her vastly underutilized human resources and dovetails best with the U.S. economy. It also is the most complicated sector to get started in, largely due to a number of institutional, governmental, and cultural factors that are discussed throughout this book. Here's a brief list of the biggest challenges:

- **Political stability:** For the most part, India's Central Government is stable. Political leadership comes from a relatively heterogeneous parliament run by a coalition of political parties. These players come from many different political arenas and have learned over the past two decades to put their differences aside and work toward common goals. Even the worst of scenarios doesn't see India falling apart, but the country could slide back far enough to hinder the pace of economic development and foreign investment interest.
- **Corruption and government interference:** India is working hard to rid itself of archaic economic and cultural policies. In the early 1990s, classic corruption and government interference had brought the nation to the brink of bankruptcy. Feudal laws and bureaucracies that paralyzed the middle class while rewarding the politically connected are now largely off the books, but many of the same unionized government bureaucrats are still punching the time clock. The state governments are not immune from criticism, either. For example, charging truckers import tariffs on the goods they carry into one state from another does little to encourage economic growth.
- **Social strife fueled by socioeconomic inequality:** The economic gap between India's poor and emerging middle class is wide. Many of India's elites are concerned that if it's not closed quickly enough, all the country's efforts at improvement will be for naught.

Small pockets of anarchic rebellion in the poorest areas have been held in check, but the spread of dissention is on every leader's mind. India's growing private sector is stepping up to the plate with job opportunities, but there's still a long way to go.

- **Functional illiteracy:** India's ultimate ability to mobilize its people and create a manufacturing economy hinges on two unrelated factors: language differences among areas of the country and inadequate education systems for the poorer people. The language differences are real and are not going away anytime soon. Much of the real effort is in teaching English at the elementary school level. However, India's educational systems have historically served the wealthy and elite of the Hindu population. Schooling in rural India is one of the Central Government's top priorities, but inefficiencies with local and state governments are hindering the implementation of education reforms.

- **Infrastructure inadequacies:** The lack of an adequate, integrated infrastructure has plagued India for many years, especially in terms of how it holds back economic growth and condemns hundreds of millions of people to a third-world existence. India recently committed huge resources to constructing the backbone of a national highway system, the Golden Quadrilateral, to complement its aging railroad network. Roads, railways, and waterways infusing the country's urban areas are now the government's top priority, and $175 billion has been budgeted through 2010 for this.

- **Inefficient banking and financial institutions:** A few U.S. and foreign commercial banks have been operating in India for several years. Foreign banks have played an important role in the banking reforms of developing country economies by providing capital to underpin the weak domestic bank sector until it can stand on its own, and to show the way toward modernization of the industry. Ideally, India would like to capitalize on this while maintaining control of its own economic destiny. After decades of protection for the banking industry, many banks are in dire straits, but the pace of reform could be much faster. The constraints on foreign investment remind many people of the old License Raj that crippled the economy for over thirty years.

- **Shifting momentum from the Central Government to the State and Union Territory Governments:** India's Central Government speaks for the nation in world affairs and provides for the national defense. At home, it knows that many of its reforms need the financial and political cooperation of the state and local governments. For example, the Central Government has moved to eliminate fiscal inefficiency by directing twenty of the largest state governments to implement a value-added tax (VAT) while it slowly eliminates the Central Sales Tax that it collects. Like all newer things in India, there are disagreements between the central and state governments on the timing and conditions of the phase-out. These could have adverse effects on economic development, such as in service taxes on some intra-state items, VAT on imports, and continued federal subsidies. Always keep in mind that succeeding in India will require you to deftly balance competing interests and seemingly contradictory requirements.

Much of the India we see today has its roots in the distant past. The subcontinent's civilization had already been waxing and waning for 3,000 years when Europeans came calling in the late fifteenth century. The Dutch and then the British established trading bases, and the latter's occupation lasted a little more than 200 years. The British replaced the Princely States, which in turn had filled the gaps left after the decline of the Mughal Empire—and so on—back in time to a thousand years before the Buddha. Today this is just a drop in the bucket for a culture as colorful and complex as that of India. Don't let blue suits and neckties fool you: Much of India has remained relatively unchanged for millennia. Her people are very good at absorbing any who come to conquer without allowing themselves to be extinguished.

Legacies of Early Empires
Anthropologists and genetic scientists place modern man in India at least 70,000 years ago, as part of the eastward migration from Africa to Australasia. Archaeologists have uncovered widespread evidence dating as early as 2500 B.C.E. of a trading network of agrarian villages along the Indus River (from which India draws its name) in what today is Pakistan.

The seeds of modern India were sown around 1500 B.C.E., when waves of foreign invaders known as Aryans entered the subcontinent through northwestern mountain passes between modern-day Pakistan and Afghanistan and spread throughout northern India. These invading civilizations brought with them a new language, Sanskrit, which evolved into Hindi, and a nature-focused religion we call Brahmanism that evolved into Hinduism. Their conquest of the north and their difference from the natives in the south created social and cultural systems that still exist today. The most notable of these are the caste and the north-south divide of languages. Gautama Buddha, who lived around 500 B.C.E., would probably recognize many things in rural Indian society today.

Ashoka and the Golden Age
The first recorded Indian imperial dynasty is that of the Maurya, who came to power in the north around 300 B.C.E. Over the next 140 years, they pushed their empire far to the south and nearly to modern Chennai and Bangalore.

Although their reign lasted only a few generations, it greatly influenced the founders of today's Republic of India. India's national emblem, the Lion Capital, is a sculpture of four lions standing back-to-back atop a pillar. This symbol is attributed to Ashoka, the greatest Mauryan king and one of the ancient world's most enduring figures. Ashoka also used the ancient Buddhist symbol of the (dharma) chakra, or twenty-four-spoke wheel of law, in many of his monuments. The Ashoka chakra is prominently depicted in the center of the Indian flag.

The Maurya Empire collapsed around 185 B.C.E., and the country settled back into disjointed kingdoms until 320 A.D., when the Gupta Empire was founded in the north. Called the Golden Age of India, the Gupta Empire was culturally one of the most important in Indian history. Gupta artists, scientists, musicians, and authors made wonderful advances in medicine, astronomy, mathematics, architecture, the arts, and literature. Gupta scientists are credited with several major discoveries that changed the world: the invention of the number zero, which formed the basis for counting by tens; knowledge that the earth was round; and the development of a 365-day calendar. They also practiced the Hindu faith and established that language and culture at India's core, where it still remains today.

The Coming of Islam

The next great change in India started in the seventh century A.D. with little fanfare. Muslim scholars, traders, and missionaries came into northern India from the Middle East and Asia in successive migrations. A few small Arab invasions took place, but for the most part the conquerors melted into oblivion. Yet over the next 300 years, they managed to fill the power vacuum left in the wake of the Gupta Empire in the Indus Valley.

During the same period, the rest of northern India saw a general decline in Indian unity among the fragmented kingdoms. This left the now-disjointed civilization unprepared for the Turkish onslaught that began in 977 A.D. Triggered by religious fervor or greed for India's rumored riches, a succession of Turkish rulers led raids into northwestern India bringing Islam with them.

By 1200 A.D., the entire north of India was under Turkish control and was being administered from the capital in Delhi. The sword of Islam had made Buddhism "extinct," and the parallel cultures of Islam and Hindu were galvanized into the villages, towns, and cities throughout India in such a way that we can still see it today. Persian literature and culture spread throughout Muslim India. Islam's intolerance of Hinduism's many gods and caste fomented religious splinter groups, the most famous of which is Sikhism.

The next great Muslim invasion to profoundly alter the subcontinent swept into India from modern Afghanistan. From 1526 through 1529, Babur defeated Indian and then Afghan leaders. He laid claim to the northern subcontinent and thus established the roots of the Mughal Empire. By the way, Mughal refers to the Mongols, as Babur is said to have descended from Genghis Khan. The English word *mogul,* which implies nearly limitless power and influence, is derived from this and was undoubtedly inspired by the vast empire the early English traders found in seventeenth-century India.

Babur did not live long enough to enjoy being the first Mughal emperor; after him, a succession of leaders saw their fortunes ebb and flow. In 1590, after twenty years of war with Hindu leaders, Akbar reconquered the north of India. Akbar is considered India's other greatest king, after Ashoka. His conquests firmly established the Mughal Empire in India and set in motion many of the things still seen in India today, such as the Urdu language, which is a blend of Persian and Hindi.

Akbar was very tolerant of other cultures and also rekindled the Hindu sprit, allowing the rebuilding of temples and monasteries. The Mughals also left an indelible mark on India with their art and architecture. We know the empire by its most famous symbol, the Taj Mahal. Completed in Agra in 1653, the Taj is the Emperor Shah Jahan's tribute to his deceased wife, Mumtaz.

The Mughal Empire also created an administrative blueprint. (A few hundred years later, the English would copy and exploit it by subduing the local Rajput kings who ruled over much of Hindu India through arranged marriages and civil appointments.) Akbar also established a formal, organized, and responsible civil service that became the administrative core of the Mughal Empire. In place at the end of the Mughal Empire were the states, languages, administrative elements, and cultural complexities that would form the Republic of India.

Great Britain and Independence

The British takeover of India began with more of a whisper than a shout. Beginning in the late 1400s, successive waves of Portuguese, Dutch, French, and British began trading along coastal India for spices, silks, and fragrances. The most famous of these early bases was Portugal's Goa, which was founded on the west coast of India in 1510 and remained in Portuguese hands for the next 450 years until India used troops to take it back in 1961. Located between the states of Maharashtra and Karnataka, Goa is still a beautiful place and a major vacation destination.

The British East India Company

England's first substantial incursions into India were on behalf of the East India Company along the southeast coasts of present day Tamil Nadu, Andhra Pradesh, and Pondicherry. In 1639, the first permanent East India Company post was established at Madras, which we all know as Chennai. The East India Company gained a second foothold on the west coast in 1668 when it received the minor Portuguese settlement of Bombay—present day Mumbai. The third and most important leg of the East India Company's tripod was acquired in 1690 when the tiny port of Calcutta was established. Calcutta, which eventually became England's first capital in India, is known today as Kolkata.

From this humble beginning, the East India Company would command its own army and use it to protect its business operations at the three ports. In 1761, the Company's army defeated the French at Pondicherry and solidified England's position as the only significant European power on the subcontinent.

Do you remember Lord Charles Cornwallis, the British commander who surrendered Yorktown to George Washington in the famous battle that finally ended British rule over the American colonies? Have you ever wondered what happened to him? Ask no more, for you're about to find out. The East India Company maintained its position in India for another twenty years by fighting battles with regional rulers around its ports. These battles firmly entrenched the British on Indian soil, but it was still a business arrangement. Cornwallis was dispatched to India by the British government for one purpose, to fold the East India Company's independent operations into a single British-run entity, which has since become known as the British Raj. This aristocrat and military general with a disdain for Indians ruthlessly went about his work. Cornwallis established systems and policies that employed only British and subjugated many Indians. These policies made conditions worse and worse until the Indians finally revolted in 1857. Their short-lived revolt was defeated in 1858 when the Indian Mutiny (the so-called Sepoy Mutiny) was finally put down. This dimmed the flames of resistance and finally established the British as the supreme rulers of Indian soil, but the embers of independence never stopped glowing.

The British Raj

The welfare of native Indians was far from the minds of the British. Foremost in their plans was establishing the systems and controls necessary to run their empire. As a result, India was stitched into a manageable unit through English surveys, roads, bridges, and administrative systems. Between 1860 and 1900, nearly 30,000 miles of railroad track were laid across the country. The British introduced education systems, hundreds of daily newspapers, telegraph systems, a postal service, modern banking systems, the rediscovery of Hindu culture, and most importantly for us, the English language.

The British also sowed the seeds of their own demise by breaking down old caste and religious prejudices that had crept back into much of daily life in the capital cities. This liberated a new national identity that would come back to haunt them. Yet their indifference to the plight of much of the population also laid the foundation for many of the biggest problems we see in India today. The antiquated agrarian economy that India is known for today was established by the British to provide products like tea, silk, and jute to the Empire. England's commercial focus on India's raw materials and use of its coffers to bolster the home government's own finances meant there was very little need for an Indian industrial base. Local merchants quickly filled this gap in the country's economy. These businessmen established family empires, such as the Tata Group and the Aditya Birla Group, that rank at the top of India's economy today.

Independence and the Nehru Legacy

1885 saw the beginning of the end of the British Raj, when a group of very wealthy and Westernized Indians formed the Indian National Congress. Started largely to express a desire for a louder voice in the running of the country, the Indian National Congress would become the core of the Indian independence movement and training ground for the leadership of the country into the twenty-first century. The children, grandchildren, and even great-grandchildren of these men would go on to become leaders and prime ministers of the future Republic of India.

Great Britain's hold on its global empire became untenable after World War II, and India's push for independence was realized on August 14, 1947. After months of negotiations with the British and with the country's Muslim leadership, India's first prime minister, Jawaharlal Nehru, proclaimed India's independence in a midnight speech to the nation. Nehru was a Hindu educated in Western schools, and he was a great admirer of the West.

Nehru also had a deep love for the poor and an inherent distrust of India's institutional discrimination. An admirer of the West, he believed that some form of democratic socialism would be the best way to improve the lot of India's people. Galvanized by India's struggle for independence and the partition of Pakistan, Nehru drew on his admiration for socialism and pushed for protectionist economic policies that would not threaten the vast majority of India's small businesses. However, at the time of Independence, most of the over 500 Princely States that had constituted much of India were still just that, feudal kingdoms ruled by princes (maharajahs). The government absorbed these states, but many of the maharajahs were allowed to keep their vast wealth and power bases intact and were granted constitutional privileges they held until 1972. The feudal systems in many of those states also stayed intact.

On January 26, 1950, India declared itself a republic. Its Constitution was based on the British parliamentary model and included a parliament, a president, and a powerful prime minister. One of the biggest challenges after Independence was to redress old grievances throughout the country. Many people still resented the presence of a strong political center and saw it as just a replacement for the British Raj. Demands for regional identity led to a redrawing of state boundaries along language-based lines. In 1956, after much effort, negotiation, and compromise, the map of India came to look much as it does today. Since then, a few of the larger states have been split again along linguistic lines; hopefully, this fragmentation is over with.

Nehru's legacy is one of great achievements and tragic failures. In his lifetime, he was able to do all of the following:

- Unify India's power brokers and common people to effect the peaceful end of the British presence.
- Oversee the transition of the country from feudal baronies to a uniform democracy.
- Identify poverty, social prejudice, women's equality, and human rights as legitimate issues for discussion and legislation. For example, the Untouchability Act (1955) was aimed squarely at ancient Hindu traditions that perpetuated the plight of India's 70 million outcastes. It also introduced controversial quotas in government service and higher education for these people.
- Pass the Hindu Marriage Act (1955) and Hindu Succession Act (1956). These two acts are considered Nehru's greatest achievements. Respectively, they established minimum ages for marriage and guaranteed women the right to divorce, and guaranteed a woman's right to inheritance of property.
- Establish a foresighted National Planning Commission to coordinate and plan India's economic development through the regular publication of five-year plans.
- Foresee India's strategic importance in Asia and help mitigate post–World War II Cold War tensions between the United States and the Soviet Union. With his nonalignment policy, Nehru declared that India would not side with one or the other and appealed to the world's smaller nations to do the same. This nonalignment movement helped eliminate the possibility of another world war by isolating the two main parties of the Cold War from many smaller nations

that would have signed non-aggression pacts in the past to ensure protection by a superpower.

Nehru himself expressed regret that he had been unable to solve some of the country's ills. Also, history would show that several of his well-intended policies weren't adequate to overcome age-old inertia in India's economic systems.

Two economic-stimulation laws, the Industries Act (1951) and the Companies Act (1956), were passed to promote industrialization. The Companies Act, which was intended to curb business monopolies, was largely ineffectual. The Industries Act, on the other hand, caused great harm. It gave the government wide-reaching powers to regulate private industry and established an all-encompassing system of licensing. Empowered by this law, government bureaucrats all but paralyzed the growth and expansion of private industry while bolstering their own importance. Corrupt local and national officials instituted open systems of bribery, whereby licenses went to the highest bidder—and some of the bids were incredibly huge. This was the now-infamous License Raj, which devastated India's middle and poor classes and extinguished much of Nehru's dreams of industrialization. Entire sectors of the economy were forced underground to avoid the pervasive red tape and inefficiency. The social and economic changes it wrought affect the Indian economy to this day.

Mostly through inaction, Nehru's governments failed to effectively contain India's growing population, which today stands around 1.1 billion people—the equivalent of Africa and South America combined.

Relations with Pakistan, Bangladesh, and China

India's fate has been intertwined with these three countries for over half a century, and this will continue into the distant future.

Partition: Pakistan and Bangladesh

By far, India's most passionate relationship is with Pakistan, which came into being in 1947 when the Indian subcontinent was partitioned along religious lines into separate Muslim and Hindu nations. The Hindu nation became India and the Muslim nation became Punjabi-controlled West Pakistan and Bengali-controlled East Pakistan.

Implementing the Partition of India was especially bloody in the north and northwest, where more than half a million people were killed when long-suppressed tensions erupted. Groups of armed civilians and paramilitary groups on both sides assaulted and attacked the Hindus traveling east into India and the Muslims traveling west into present-day Pakistan—an estimated 5 million migrants.

Violence threatened to become equally devastating in Bengal, where 500,000 Hindus, Muslims, and Sikhs were relocating between the new East Pakistan and India. Only a hunger strike "to the death" by Mahatma Gandhi was sufficient to quell the violence in Bengal, although it was too late to undo what had been done in the west. It was Gandhi's role in suppressing the violence that led to his assassination by a Hindu extremist on January 30, 1948.

Kashmir and More Bloodshed

Tensions in the west remained high. When the Hindu maharajah of the state of Kashmir waffled on his decision to join India in 1947, preferring to remain independent, his Muslim subjects revolted. They were supported by a group of West Pakistani militants, who invaded the kingdom and threatened to take it over. The maharajah appealed to India for help and troops were sent to drive out the invaders, even though the majority of Kashmiris were Muslim. The troops drove the invaders back into the western part of Kashmir, and the final battle line between the two armies formed an unofficial and disputed border between the two countries. In 1949, the United Nations inserted a peacekeeping mission that remains to this day. Today, about 35 percent of Kashmir lies in Pakistani control, while the remaining 65 percent forms the Indian state of Jammu and Kashmir. Since 1948, numerous skirmishes and two more wars have broken out between the countries.

In 1965, war again broke out. West Pakistan and India bombed each other's cities, and battles were fought along the countries' borders and in the Indian state of Punjab. The conflict brought the world near the brink of war when China threatened to intervene, but China backed down in the face of pressure by the United States and Great Britain. Again, the United Nations brokered a peace agreement and a still-disputed border, the Line of Control, was established.

Bangladesh, Indira Gandhi, and the Soviet Union

In 1971, tensions over the distribution of resources between West Pakistan and East Pakistan erupted when a pro-Bengali administration was elected to power in East Pakistan. West Pakistan sent troops to remove the administration, and a bloody civil war ensued. Indira Gandhi, Nehru's daughter and India's untested prime minister, received her baptism by fire during this conflict. Her decisiveness and deft management of the conflict when it spilled over into India firmly established her as the leader of the nation. India soundly defeated Pakistan, and East Pakistan became Bangladesh.

At the war's height, 10 million refugees had fled East Pakistan to India. Over the next year, the refugees returned home without incident. The ensuing political turmoil in Pakistan allowed Zulfikar Ali Bhutto to take control of the country, and it formally recognized Bangladesh in 1974. Interestingly, the United States and China were in West Pakistan's camp during this conflict while the Soviet Union, which had just signed a twenty-year treaty of peace and cooperation with New Delhi, took the Indian side.

During the conflict, the United States mobilized the Seventh Fleet to the Bay of Bengal. Gandhi, using her clout with the Soviets, did not back down and brought the conflict under control and to a quick end. Ghandi's pact with the Soviet Union would cloud U.S.-India relations for years to come. In some ways, it also kept India from entering the world stage as an equal player.

The Soviet Union's invasion of Afghanistan in 1979 to suppress a civil rebellion put an unplanned strain on India-Pakistan relations. Pakistan sided with the Afghan rebels. India, because of its 1971 treaty, took the Soviet side. India and Pakistan maintained a strategic dialogue over the following eight years that concluded with the countries' agreeing not to attack each other's nuclear power plants, which initiated further agreements on cultural exchanges and civil aviation. In 2004, India and Pakistan agreed to restart talks on peace and security in Jammu and Kashmir. Also on the table were technical and secretary-level discussions on six other bilateral disputes: Siachen Glacier, Wuller Barrage/Tulbul Navigation Project, Sir Creek estuary, terrorism, drug trafficking, economic and commercial cooperation, and the promotion of friendly exchanges in various fields.

An Optimistic Future

All in all, the atrocities that occurred during Partition greatly contributed to the longstanding mistrust and animosity between India and Pakistan. Now, sixty years later, most of the people who were involved are no longer alive, and both nations are cautiously looking forward to a peaceful and more prosperous future. In 1985, both countries became founding members of the South Asian Association of Regional Cooperation (SAARC), which encourages cooperation in agriculture, rural development, science and technology, culture, health, population control, narcotics, and terrorism. Members of SAARC include Bangladesh,

Bhutan, India, Maldives, Nepal, Pakistan, and Sri Lanka. SAARC also accords observer status to the United States, the European Union, China, Japan, and South Korea. SAARC currently serves as a forum for dialogue among its member nations as well as its observer nations. SAARC member nations are signatories to the 2006 South Asia Free Trade Agreement (SAFTA), which reduces tariffs on interregional trade between SAARC member nations.

Trade between India and Pakistan has historically been small, amounting to less than 1 percent of each country's import/export business. Data shows, however, that trade has been on the increase:

- $161 million in 1999–2000
- $345 million in 2003–2004
- $602 million in 2004–2005

In addition to diplomatic efforts from New Delhi, India's commercial center of Mumbai is taking an active role in opening new ties between the two countries' business communities by aligning itself as much as possible with Karachi in Pakistan. An independent business think-tank has been created with the full support of the Karachi Chamber of Commerce and Industry and the Maharashtra Economic Development Council. There is still talk within some Pakistani business circles about their fear of the much larger Indian economy, so India will have to work to dispel these concerns. Following the October 2005 earthquake in Kashmir, India and Pakistan coordinated relief efforts. The countries opened access points along the Line of Control to allow relief supplies to flow from India to Pakistan, and to enable Kashmiris from both sides to visit each other. Finally, the United States has forged stronger ties with both nations, a diplomatic commonality that cannot but help see them over the hump.

Relations with China

Americans love to debate the relative merits and short-comings of India and China. Conversations routinely devolve to the standard bromides: India is best positioned to exploit the high-tech market, while China has the manufacturing base to grow into the twenty-first century; intellectual property rights are suspect in China, while India's use of English puts it in good position for American businesses. Are these statements true, or are we Americans simplifying things into headline format? Regardless of how we view these countries, the more important question concerns how they view each other.

Toward Open Trade

Despite some minor saber-rattling in the past, India and China have begun to position themselves for leadership roles in Asia. Together they account for four out of every ten people on earth. Both have been able to tap into their vast human resources to sustain economic growth at rates approaching double–digits. Most importantly, both see merit in investing in each other's economy. China has been the more aggressive suitor and for several years has been pushing for a free-trade agreement. India's reply to these advances has been lukewarm. Both countries signed a limited trade agreement in 1984 and still see pluses and minuses in an open-trade arrangement, although India will get the short end of the stick, for now. This is because most trade agreements primarily focus on reducing import and export barriers to goods as opposed to services. The Indian economy is 54 percent services, 28 percent manufacturing, and 18 percent agriculture; the Chinese economy, on the other hand, is roughly 33 percent services and over 50 percent manufacturing, with the remainder devoted to agriculture. Nearly half of India's exports to China are raw materials, while the majority of imports from China are manufactured goods.

In essence, then, India sees free trade as a one-way street for the rupee, with manufactured goods coming into the subcontinent but very little in the way of manufactured goods moving out.

India is desperately trying to jump-start its manufacturing sector, and the perception is that free flow of Chinese manufactured products would harm these efforts. As a developing nation, India has more freedom to keep its import tariffs high. In contrast, China had to lower its import tariffs in a compromise measure to gain entry to the World Trade Organization.

Business Sectors Showing Promise

A recent FICCI straw poll of Indian officials and business leaders identified the following sectors as key areas for India-China cooperation: energy, biotechnology, information and communication technology, pharmaceuticals, and financial services. China is India's second-largest trading partner—behind the United States and ahead of the United Arab Emirates—and India is China's largest Asian trading partner. Here are some recent trade numbers for the two countries:

- 1999: $2 billion
- 2003: $8 billion
- 2004: $14 billion
- 2005: $17 billion
- 2006: $25 billion

China's ambassador to India was quoted in the March 31, 2005, issue of *Asia Times* as suggesting that the two countries have the potential to reach $35 billion in trade by 2010 and could even reach $50 billion, if all trade barriers were dropped. India is quick to point out that the current balance of trade is in China's favor. The countries do have gentlemen's agreements in place to broaden mutual cooperation in agriculture, dairy, and fisheries. India, however, is concerned about transparency and intellectual property rights in China's economy. At the same time, Indian service companies like Infosys have done projects in China, and Chinese companies have set up limited operations in India in the form of representative offices to support marketing efforts and project offices to support infrastructure contracts. In fact, India has become a preferred destination for Chinese contracting companies.

Despite their on-again, off-again trade overtures, India and China have linked forces to participate is several energy joint ventures in Africa. Both countries are likely to continue to leverage their positions in Africa and Latin America towards other developing markets while they decide who will lead and who will follow on the big dance floor.

Relations with the United States

Until recently, the relationship between the United States and India was not very close; it was even somewhat strained from 1971 to 1991. During that time, events such as India's alignment with the Soviet Union during the Pakistani civil war in Bangladesh did little to assuage the tensions. Critical differences remained, such as those over India's nuclear weapons programs and the pace of India's economic reforms.

In the past, those concerns dominated U.S. thinking about India; today, the United States views India as a growing economic power in the world and is refraining from big-stick diplomacy. The nuclear nonproliferation dialogue initiated after India's 1998 nuclear tests has bridged many of the gaps in understanding between the countries. In 2001, the United States lifted sanctions, which were imposed under the terms of the 1994 Nuclear Proliferation Prevention Act following India's nuclear tests in May 1998. The United States recognizes India as its key strategic partner in the region and has worked to strengthen their relationship. The countries have demonstrated a common interest in the free flow of commerce and resources, including through the vital sea lanes of the Indian Ocean, and also share an interest in fighting terrorism and in creating a strategically stable Asia.

High-level meetings and committed cooperation between the two countries increased during 2002 and 2003. In January 2004, the United States and India launched the Next Steps in Strategic Partnership (NSSP), which was a milestone in the transformation of the bilateral relationship and served as a blueprint for future discussions. The completion of Phase I of the NSSP included implementing measures to address nuclear proliferation concerns and to ensure compliance with U.S. export controls.

These efforts have enabled the United States to make modifications to its export licensing policies that will foster cooperation in commercial space programs and permit certain exports to power plants at safeguarded nuclear facilities. These modifications include removing the Indian Space Research Organization (ISRO) Headquarters from the Department of Commerce Entity List. In January 2004, the United States and India agreed to expand cooperation in three specific areas: civilian nuclear activities, civilian space programs, and high-technology trade. In addition, the two countries agreed to expand their dialogue on missile defense. These areas of cooperation are designed to progress through a series of reciprocal steps that build on each other. To be successful, both countries must remain committed and productive to this process.

In 2005, both countries announced agreements that further enhanced these areas of cooperation as well as other initiatives: a U.S.-India economic dialogue, the fight against HIV/AIDS, disaster relief, technology cooperation, a democracy initiative, the Agriculture Knowledge Initiative, a trade policy forum, an energy dialogue, and a CEO forum.

In December 2006, the U.S. Congress passed the U.S.-India Peaceful Atomic Energy Cooperation Act, which allows direct civilian nuclear commerce with India for the first time in 30 years. This legislation cleared the way for India to buy U.S. nuclear reactors and fuel for civilian use. The United States and India are seeking to elevate the strategic partnership further to include cooperation in counter-terrorism, defense cooperation, education, and joint democracy promotion.

Trade Pacts

India has been very active in courting the nations of the world for trade. In addition to the United States, India is pursuing opportunities in Latin America and Africa as part of the South-South initiatives, and with the Association of South East Asian Nations (ASEAN) as part of its Look East initiative. Numerous countries have signed various types of agreements with India, and others are lining up to do the same. Here is a list of the major bilateral trade agreement vehicles that India is party to:

Comprehensive Economic Cooperation Agreements
India-Singapore CECA

Framework Agreements
Framework Agreement with ASEAN
Framework Agreement with Chile
Framework Agreement with the states of the Gulf Cooperation Council
Framework Agreement with Thailand

Free Trade Agreements
India-Sri Lanka Free Trade Agreement

Joint Study Groups
India-Korea Joint Study Group

Preferential Trade Agreements
India-Afghanistan Preferential Trade Agreements
India-Chile Preferential Trade Agreements

India-MERCOSUR Preferential Trade Agreements (MERCOSUR is a South American free-trade agreement involving Argentina, Brazil, Chile, Paraguay, and Uruguay)

Strategic Partnership Joint Action Plans
India-EU Strategic Partnership Joint Action Plan

Trade Agreements
India-Bangladesh Trade Agreement
India-Bhutan Trade Agreement
India-Ceylon Trade Agreement
India-China Trade Agreement
India-DPR Korea Trade Agreement
India-Japan Trade Agreement
India-Korea Trade Agreement
India-Maldives Trade Agreement
India-Mongolia Trade Agreement
India-Pakistan Trade Agreement

Trade Treaties
India-Nepal Trade Treaty

The Central Government provides the most current trade pact information on the Ministry of Commerce and Industry Web site (online at *www.commerce.nic.in/*).

High Expectations

Since the country won its independence in 1950, India's National Planning Commission has been publishing five-year plans more or less on schedule. Prompted in part by the findings of the United Nations and its proposed Millennium Development Goals for India, the planning commission constituted the Committee on Vision 2020 in June 2000. The committee came to realize that India needed a true strategic vision instead of another hopeful wish list of goals that were nearly impossible to achieve. In doing so, the government's honesty with itself is an inspiration to all of the country's people, challenging them to set aside their differences and work together to make India a great nation.

The committee's framework report identified many important issues, but the two it emphasized as most crucial to India's success are employment and education. In order to eradicate malnutrition and other health-related issues, 200 million new jobs will have to be created by 2020. Eliminating illiteracy and educating young people to fill the jobs of the twenty-first century will require enrolling all children in primary schools and guarantees for secondary education and job training for all Indians.

The report also examines issues related to population growth, food production, health, vulnerable sections of the population, transportation, communications, energy self-sufficiency, water conservation and air quality, trade investment, peace, security, and governance. Its conclusion is that India has the opportunity to emerge as one of the world's leading economies during the next twenty years, provided her citizens have the self-confidence, the self-reliance, and the determination to realize their individual and collective potentials.

An Overview of Business in India

The U.S. State Department's Bureau of South and Central Asian Affairs estimates that India's population is nearly 1.1 billion and is growing at 1.3 percent a year. India has the world's twelfth-largest economy—and the third-largest in Asia, behind Japan and China—with a total gross domestic product (GDP) around $1 trillion. The World Trade Organization puts India's GDP purchasing power parity (PPP) at over $4 trillion. Services, industry, and agriculture account for 54 percent, 28 percent, and 18 percent of GDP respectively. There is a large and growing middle class estimated at 325 million people. Nearly two-thirds of the population depends on agriculture for its livelihood and lives on less than $2 per day. About 34 percent of the population lives on less than $1 per day.

Reforms

India is continuing to move forward with market-oriented economic reforms that began in 1991. Recent reforms include liberalized foreign investment and exchange regimes, industrial decontrol, reductions in tariffs and other trade barriers, reform and modernization of the financial sector, adjustments in government monetary and fiscal policies, and safeguarding of intellectual property rights.

Real GDP growth for the fiscal year ending March 31, 2006, was 8.4 percent, up from the 7.7 percent growth of the previous year. Foreign portfolio and direct investment inflows have significantly risen in recent years. They have contributed to the $166 billion in foreign exchange reserves by mid-September 2006. Government receipts from privatization were about $3 billion in fiscal year (FY) 2003–2004. However, economic growth is constrained by inadequate infrastructure, a cumbersome bureaucracy, corruption, labor market rigidities, regulatory and foreign investment controls, the "reservation" of key products for small-scale industries, and high fiscal deficits. The outlook for further trade liberalization is mixed. India eliminated quotas on 1,420 consumer imports in 2002 and has announced its intention to continue to lower customs duties. However, the tax structure is complex, with compounding effects of various taxes.

International Trade

The United States is India's largest trading partner. Bilateral trade in 2005 was $26.8 billion. Principal U.S. exports are diagnostic and laboratory reagents, aircraft and aircraft parts, advanced machinery, cotton, fertilizers, ferrous waste/scrap metal, and computer hardware. Major U.S. imports from India include textiles and ready-made garments, Internet-enabled services, agricultural and related products, gems and jewelry, leather products, chemicals, and other consumer goods.

The rapidly growing software sector is boosting service exports and modernizing much of India's economy. Revenues from the information technology (IT) industry reached $23.6 billion in FY 2005–2006. Software exports exceeded $22 billion in FY 2005–2006. IT and business process outsourcing (BPO) exports are projected to grow by nearly 30 percent during FY 2006–2007. Personal computer usage is 14 per 1,000 persons, although much of this is likely to be IT and BPO work-related. The cellular/mobile telephone market served 140 million subscribers as of November 2006. The country has 54 million cable TV customers.

Foreign Investment and Development Assistance

The United States is India's largest investment partner, with a 13 percent share. India's total inflow of U.S. direct investment is estimated at more than $5 billion through FY 2005–2006. Some industrial sectors are still closed to foreign investment, as are government-owned businesses such as Indian Railways and Air India. Foreign investment is particularly sought after in power generation, telecommunications, ports, roads, petroleum exploration/processing, and mining.

India's external debt was $125 billion in FY 2005–2006, up from $123 billion in FY 2004–2005. Foreign assistance was approximately $3.8 billion in FY 2005–2006, with the United States providing about $126 million in development assistance. The World Bank plans to double aid to India to almost $3 billion a year, with a focus on infrastructure, education, health, and rural livelihoods.

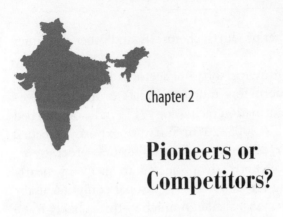

Chapter 2

Pioneers or Competitors?

It's around now that you'll need to start thinking about what you want to get out of your Indian venture. Will it be to buy and hold for several years and then to sell at a profit at some future date? Perhaps your vision is to gain a foothold in the country with a small investment that you can grow through diverse acquisitions. Or is flipping investments your forte? Regardless of what you're planning, are you ready for the realities of doing business in a very foreign country? How much should you know about the companies you'll be investing in and doing business with?

Stories abound about the gold rush of foreign direct-investment into India. A quick read of these stories paints images eerily similar to much of what was published about the dot-com boom during the 1990s. In fact, many journalists are purposely drawing parallels and using similar terms, such as "bursting bubbles." Are these two phenomena the same? Are investors in India fated to play the same game of musical chairs? It takes some reading between the lines to understand the differences. This little bit of research also sheds light on the real India, which is vastly different from what many would ask us to believe. Understanding and accepting the real India will go a long way toward ensuring the success of your project or venture.

Consider the current rush for foreign investment in India and the dot-com boom of the 1990s. In both cases, investment came largely in the form of speculation. Buyers looked first to cheaply acquire assets and worried later about what to do with them. After the first wave of investments in the IT and telecom sectors, many of the Indian firms targeted were small- and medium-sized family owned businesses in a wider range of sectors that serviced much of the new business traffic and upcoming middle class. But how much is known about these businesses? Once acquired, will U.S. management styles and goals improve the business, hurt it, or simply not make any difference? Is the responsiveness to change of Indian companies, employees, and the business environment similar to what we're used to here in the United States?

The National Inertia

India is commonly symbolized by the elephant. In many ways, the elephant is an appropriate symbol for Old India. Very large and very heavy, it moves gracefully but slowly. Only the elephant itself is strong enough to alter its speed or change its direction. Its uniform tone camouflages flaws and defies the casual observer to find and focus on details. It is very intelligent, very social, and very vegetarian. Elephants live long lives and are remembered long after they're gone. Yet, like the elephant, Old India often allowed uninspired drivers to steer it hither, thither, and yon in the performance of routine and mundane tasks. The strength of its people was exploited, and its ivory harvested and shipped overseas.

Thankfully, those days are coming to an end. Now, half a century after Independence, many Indians are looking far beyond the coastline for inspiration and metrics to compare their country with. We're seeing some of the old paradigms fall by the wayside as enlightened Indians, both young and old, blaze new trails and forge vastly different futures for themselves and their families. Still, many of India's entrenched institutions, social mores, and cultural systems will resist changing direction. Like the elephant, this course correction can only be accomplished from within. Taking a little time to develop an awareness of two institutions, the bureaucratic Raj and business classifications, will greatly benefit the American businessperson's decision-making and help him or her identify unusual opportunities.

Remnants of the License Raj

License Raj is a sarcastic term that refers to the overbearing, unfair, undemocratic system of overt corruption that permeated Indian business and government for nearly forty years. Although many of the official policies that contributed to its existence were abolished in the 1980s and 1990s, the underlying causes and prejudices are still around and continue to cause inefficiencies in many areas of the economy. A recent example of this can be seen in two *Daily Telegraph* (*www .telegraph.co.uk*) articles by Peter Foster.

Mr. Foster tells the tale of how India's minister of railways refused to allow imports of rail-carriage wheels from the United States, China, and Germany. The railroad, which is totally owned and operated by the government, is poorly maintained and suffers an accident with injuries nearly every day. It was hoped that modernizing the system would help improve its safety record and efficiency. Despite the pressing need for new railcars, the minister refused to sanction imports of any kind. Instead, he proposed that a wheel manufacturing plant be constructed in his home state of Bihar, which is India's poorest. The minister reasoned that producing the wheels in India had "merit" for the country's people and also pointed out that Vishwakarma, the Hindu god of machines, is ultimately responsible for the railroad.

The first reason harkens back to the ill-conceived socialist policies that condemned the country to backwardness for over a generation. The second reason is absurd by Western standards, although plausible within the Indian consciousness.

Ultimately, criticism for this decision focused directly on the protectionist legacy of the License Raj as the major cause.

Backbone of the Bureaucratic System

The term *Raj* has evolved into use as a metaphor for any widespread bureaucratic system. How did the License Raj work in everyday life? Changing or starting a new industrial business almost universally meant the need to obtain one or more licenses, which were issued by local bureaucrats. If your connections weren't good, you might have to pay large bribes and wait six months or longer, because "all of the available licenses for that sector are already accounted for." If you wanted to expand an existing business, you needed to queue up for a license and an eighteen-month wait.

While you waited, well-connected businesses easily obtained permits for their endeavors, reinforcing pandemic political cronyism and corruption throughout the country. For example, in the mid-1980s, an associate of mine took advantage of government initiatives to start a manufacturing business. Every day, for weeks on end, he sat in the local licensing-and-permitting office waiting to see an official so he could apply for a license. While waiting, he sat and watched as the favored local business elite walked in and out of the office, obtaining whatever they wanted. But he never gave up and, after weeks of sitting all day in that office, he was granted his license.

The License Raj wasn't the only culprit choking economic growth and opportunity for many would-be entrepreneurs. For example, suppose a poor monsoon rainfall left reservoirs with low water levels, which meant less electricity or available cooling water for your manufacturing plant. Operating far below design capacity translated to lost sales and lost revenues. Many of your workers were idled—but they were still being paid because you could not lay anyone off without the proper bureaucratic authorization. Sensing your plight, the government offered subsidies to ensure that you stayed in business—subsidies drawn from rapidly emptying public coffers. Benevolent and hands-off practices like these, along with poorly managed foreign and domestic borrowing, took the country to the brink of bankruptcy in 1991.

History of the License Raj

How did the License Raj arise? Following Independence, the new leadership of India was determined to promote industrialization and economic self-sufficiency through the protection of domestic industry and socialist policies. Reliance on capitalist imports was viewed as harmful to growth and contrary to the country becoming economically independent and were shunned through outright bans or protectionist tariffs. The government passed two laws, the Industries Act and the Companies Act, which led to a complex system of licensing and permitting that was quickly abused by the bureaucrats and their well-connected cronies to gain and hold control over local and regional domestic economies. New industries had great difficulty getting started and, more critically, new product innovation was stalled. The results were a spectacularly corrupt bureaucracy and an incredibly inefficient macroeconomy that lasted an entire generation from the 1950s until the 1980s, when it became embarrassingly clear that the protectionist policies weren't working. The government finally saw fit to start phasing them out, but enormous pressure brought by the beneficiaries of corruption at all levels in the country caused the problems to drag on for years.

The middle and lower classes, unwilling to subscribe to a socialist system that rewarded the well connected while subjugating everyone else, have found all sorts of ways to get around the laws. They operate on the honor system and conduct barter transactions. Firms resorted to creating their own currency to conduct business. Huge numbers of informal businesses sprung up to serve the public demand. Taxes could not be calculated or collected. An entirely independent culture and economy arose and still flourishes.

The License Raj created or contributed to several wide-spread and long-lasting effects. It is responsible for the following:

- Contributing to an overall domestic malaise that saw "Main Street" India miss out on the opportunities that many Southeast Asian countries used to build manufacturing bases.
- Establishing an irresponsible, self-perpetuating bureaucracy that still exists throughout much of the country.
- Giving birth to a generation of uncompetitive, poorly performing businesses that may not survive India's new economic expansion.
- Crippling domestic productivity that has failed to keep pace with the country's growing population.
- Engendering an anti-regulatory, anti-government mindset that still jeopardizes government initiatives and needed improvements in many sectors.

Legacy of the License Raj

Although the License Raj has been formally absent from industrial development for over twenty-five years, critics point to similar policies that still exist in other public institutions, such as elementary and higher education. It appears that this is shaping up as one of the next big battlegrounds between the traditionalists and the reformers.

A new Raj, the Inspection Raj, is being bandied about in print and electronic media. The Inspection Raj is characterized by increasingly frequent and picayune visits to industrial facilities by state and local inspectors, who often find arcane or absurd problems that need "correction." Needless to say, most of these problems are fixed in the traditional way. Proponents of the practice point toward India's crumbling infrastructure and public health systems as proof that inspections are crucial to maintain the country's progress. Critics are passionate that the practice stifles business development and economic progress while perpetuating corruption and inefficiency. It's likely there is merit in the arguments of both sides and, hopefully, progress won't suffer while the debate rages on.

The Organized and Unorganized Sectors

We've seen how the License Raj helped galvanize small businesses and family businesses away from the formal government. For the most part, bureaucrats were unconcerned about this, because their primary focus was on perpetuating their own jobs. As a result, you will find significant grey areas in demographic data. One of the most confusing things you will encounter when trying to digest Indian industrial data is the classification of businesses. In India, all businesses fall into one of two categories: those in the Organized (or Formal) Sector, and everything else. As the name suggests, there are businesses, services, and employees whose activities are traceable or are registered with one or another form of government agency. By default, everything else comprises what is called the Unorganized, or Informal, Sector.

The Organized Sector

The Central Government only collects economic data on the Organized Sector. As a result, all official government statistics, such as unemployment and personal income, are limited in applicability and interpretation. The standard industrial classifications that U.S. managers are so familiar with only apply to the Organized Sector. All other published data are just government guesses. The following are examples of entities that are part of the Organized Sector:

- Services run by the government (Central, state, and local) and all its agencies
- Manufacturing companies covered under the government's Annual Survey of Industries

- Large business organizations and public, private, and private limited corporations with ten or more employees (a proposed definition)
- Small industrial businesses registered with various District Industries Centers
- Cottage industries registered with the Khadi and Village Industries Commission
- Small-scale businesses registered under the Shops and Establishments Act of 1953

What is not always evident is that there is no single, official definition for a business in the Organized Sector. It varies from state to state, region to region, industry to industry, and even size to size.

The Unorganized Sector

What does the Unorganized Sector look like? Typical jobs and employers are seasonal construction workers, farm laborers, and skilled and unskilled workers in very small businesses. Typical entrepreneurs in this sector are small roadside shopkeepers, sidewalk vendors, small agriculturalists, direct-sales representatives, and tiny cottage businesses being run from virtually anywhere.

The relative sizes of these two sectors is staggering. According to the U.S. Department of State, of India's nearly 496 million workers, only 7 percent (34.7 million) are employed in the Organized Sector; of these, between 65 percent and 70 percent are public service employees. The other 461 million working Indians literally fall through the cracks! Here are some other facts about the Indian workforce:

- 80 percent of all working Indians do not receive a formal paycheck.
- 65 percent of all Indians make their livelihoods from small businesses in the agricultural sector.

- 92 percent of all women workers are employed in the Unorganized Sector.
- India is the world's largest milk producer, yet only 15 percent of dairy-related businesses are organized.
- Labor in the Organized Sector comprises as little as 1.5 percent of the total labor economy.

Effects of Economic Growth

Growth in the Organized Sector is generally sluggish. This is attributed to archaic labor laws, which restrict downsizing and encourage hiring contract workers instead of full-time employees, and gender bias against women. Between 2005 and 2006, the employment rates in the industrial (17 percent), agricultural (60 percent), and services (23 percent) sectors did not change, while the overall number of workers increased 2.9 percent from 482 million to 496 million. Presumably, these 14 million new workers found employment somewhere in the Unorganized Sector.

The ramifications of this are critical as India struggles to get its arms around the fundamental issues and initiatives of job creation and social security. Furthermore, concerns about the future competitiveness of the Indian small-business (Unorganized) economy are being raised, due to its historic lack of access to raw materials, business finance, technology and technical skills, entrepreneurship development, infrastructure, and domestic markets.

Interestingly, many of India's new software startups are in the Unorganized Sector, presumably because of their small size and ability to sidestep many of the traditional constraints put on the Organized Sector. For example, software firms do not have to worry about sourcing raw materials, developing markets, or using roadways and railroads to produce and deliver their products. Instead of employees, they can retain contract workers who can be cut loose as soon as a project is completed. Not falling into large-company categories or standard industrial classifications enables them to reduce reporting requirements. As was discussed earlier in this chapter, Indians like to fly under the radar.

Opportunities for American Investors

What do these demographics mean to the disciplined U.S. investor? There are many uncut diamonds out there, and thorough due diligence should help uncover them. It's important to stay as personally involved in the search as possible and to resist jumping at the first can't-miss opportunity.

In many cases, finding the right match may take a little longer, but it should be worth the wait. This is where face-to-face meetings and negotiations with your Indian counterpart are crucial, as the ultimate success or failure of your venture will depend on forming a trusting business, and even personal, relationship. Here are some things to keep an eye out for. The business that an agent or broker shows you may not have any tax records or legitimate income records. Or perhaps those being shown to you are pure fabrications. Many of a business's records of transactions with other businesses may be inaccurate, or the transactions may have gone unrecorded. Employees may come and go as seasonal or family duties call. A firm's payables may consist of little more than IOUs and promissory notes for future favors, instead of recourse to hard cash. The list of potential pitfalls is real. Don't be discouraged, because the rewards can more than make up for a little temporary frustration.

Alternative Approaches to Empowering Individuals

Every successful negotiator knows that being able to determine what people want is the shortest route to a win–win situation. Yet, if asked what we want, many of us might draw a blank or feebly offer up desires for whatever happens to be perched atop our consciousness stack at that moment. Obviously, we need to be led in the proper direction, which is what proficient salespeople are very good at.

You may wonder what this has to do with India. Well, you may have heard or read about the similarities and differences between Indians and Americans. One that is offered up fairly frequently is, "Americans live to work, while Indians work to live."

Quite a generalization, isn't it? We all know that Americans don't live to work, although we do take pride in our ability to pull together as a team to overcome crises and obstacles, and we often see our work as an important extension of ourselves. "What do you do?" is probably the most-asked question when meeting someone new. There's an underlying, important message here that says, "It's good to live for something."

Dale Carnegie emphasized this fundamental desire to be important and wrote about it as one of the two most critical human needs. The same needs and desires hold true for the billion residents of India. They, however, tend to define their sense of self-worth much more along cultural, rather than individual, lines. Family, caste, and community are far more important in the average Indian's life than they are in the average American's. In that respect, most Indians do work to live. The quality of the average Indian's life, however, has been very different from the average American's. Despite these differences, a new class of Indian salesperson is emerging whose products are ideas, not goods or services.

Starting in 1991 and accelerating ever since, cracks have begun to appear in the foundations of some of India's traditional institutions. Parents, for example, no longer have the exclusive right to plan and facilitate marriages. Systems of higher education are coming under increased pressure to flush out old, staid ideas and make room for the poor and underprivileged. Many highly educated and successful Indians who had emigrated for personal reasons have begun to return home with new and revolutionary, for India, ideas. They are questioning the status quo while proposing new approaches to business and education, which they believe will enable India to bootstrap itself and its people into a global leadership role. They also see the United States as their strategic partner in this evolution. While not very new to most Americans, these ideas are somewhat radical for traditional Indians and should be evaluated in that context. Some of their points are worth examining:

- Many Indians wake up each day with no opportunity for advancement or reason for taking personal initiatives. The former comes from a very real and rigid social structure, while the latter is the psychological result of a life where whatever one does makes little difference.
- Government-mandated reverse discrimination quotas and reservations, while well-meaning and better than doing nothing, may not be the most effective way to stabilize the population and lay a strong foundation for the future. The means to overcome these barriers are through increasing self-awareness and understanding self-worth.
- Every individual's personal growth and wealth should come from altruistic, creative, and contributory work and not from the exploitation of others or others' resources.
- The Raj-like manipulation of social and economic systems for one's own benefit destroys the potential for creating win-win opportunities that increase every individual's wealth and, ultimately, the nation's well-being.
- The challenge to leadership at all levels is to create opportunities for all Indians, above and beyond everything else.

By focusing on "knowledge-driven commerce" and exposing the futility of "commerce-driven knowledge," these leaders are breaking new ground with alternative approaches to empowering Indian individuals through innovative educational and personal-improvement training. I believe their future is bright.

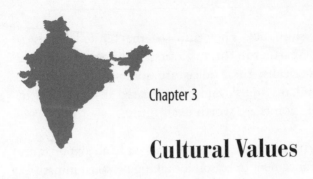

Chapter 3

Cultural Values

It might be difficult for an American businessperson to fully grasp the intricacies and importance that culture plays in an Indian's everyday life. Failure to do so could mean the difference between success and collapse for your venture. This is further complicated by the rapid changes brought on by business growth that are taking place throughout certain areas of the country. However, a Western businessperson with experience in South Asia or Japan is more likely to discover that the rigidity of Indian culture is vaguely familiar.

Regardless of creed, region, or economic well-being, traditional Indian culture is founded on a fairly strict social hierarchy wherein every individual's place can be defined by birth, wealth, power, age, and gender, all of which are tightly woven into a social tapestry that transcends space and time. From their earliest years, individuals are taught and reminded of their roles and places in society, to the point that their core identities are forged from it.

Without this identity as a starting point, it's often difficult and could be nearly impossible for an individual to develop a sense of self-worth and become acceptable to the rest of society. Even worse, one would most certainly not have a social safety net of family and friends from which to draw upon to provide for personal needs, assistance, and support. Thus, most Indians spend a huge amount of time and energy—disproportional by Western standards—nurturing and maintaining their social bonds within the hierarchy.

This system is further reinforced by traditional and ancient religious beliefs. For many traditional Indians, the ancient gods and spirits are literally alive and serving an integral and functional role in their relationships and personal well-being. The Indian culture is optimized to function this way. This point cannot be stressed too strongly.

Religion and Occupation: Defining Society

The keen observer of traditional Indian society will notice several differentiators that should always be kept in mind. One is religion. The vast majority of Indians are either Hindu or Muslim. Interestingly, like here in the West, this difference is not as divisive as one might at first think.

The other and far more powerful differentiator is occupation. Traditional Hindu society is bifurcated into individuals who perform clean (or "non-polluting") work and those who perform unclean (or polluting) work. Although these two groups have functioned symbiotically—or parasitically, if one takes the moral high ground—for thousands of years, the strict social taboos that govern their interrelationships are quite alien to Westerners.

Consider these typical American jobs: the butcher at your local supermarket; the transportation employee who occasionally collects animal carcasses from the sides of roads and highways; undertakers; taxidermists; fish mongers; workers in animal husbandry; trash collectors; pig, chicken, turkey, cow, and horse farmers; and zookeepers. In traditional India, all these individuals work in unclean or polluting jobs. Along with their families and kin, they may be viewed and treated poorly by the other side of traditional Hindu society. Remember the 1950s hit television show *The Honeymooners*? In a traditionally strict Indian community, the popularity of this program would be unthinkable because a bus driver and his family could not socialize with a sewer worker and his family. These traditions, while on the wane in growing areas like the big cities, still burn violently hot in the more secluded regions of India.

Obviously, in a country as stratified as India, geography and demographics influence the degree and flexibility of this hierarchy. Thankfully, in modern times and for some individuals, lines between adjacent levels in the hierarchy are blurring and, in some instances, disappearing altogether. However, the astute visitor will err on the side of caution in social settings until the big picture reveals itself.

Family Values

To a far greater degree than in the West, the family is the nuclear group for the majority of Indian society, regardless of religion or economic status. The family unit is further buttressed by cooperative kinship relationships, usually defined by marriage. From birth through adolescence, adult life, and death, Indians look first and foremost to the family structure for support and guidance. In return, the family and related kinships function and survive largely through loyalty from their members. It should come as no surprise, then, to learn that many of India's strongest and most successful businesses are family and kinship based, having survived for generations through mutual cooperation and respect for the social structure.

The vast majority of Indian family relationships are traceable for generations through the male line from fathers to sons, grandsons, and even great-grandsons. Along with their wives and children, these "joint" families and their kin form the core of India's society. When a woman marries, she leaves her parent's home and goes to live with her husband. In this way, a family can grow quite large and powerful. After marriage, women still retain strong ties to their own families, which forms one basis for kinship in India. Other kinships grow out of strong ties between close male relatives and even other male friends, not unlike the bonds made in college-based fraternities. Like all Indian kinship relationships, even these require constant attention to personal and social obligations.

Still larger than the family is the *gotra,* a clannish designation given at birth and usually the same as that of the male parent. Unlike the family with its obvious biological roots, the *gotra* is largely shrouded in myth and traces its lineage back to ancient, seminal ancestors. Regardless of its mysterious origins, the *gotra* plays a crucial role in Hindu marriage. Put simply, marriage or even sexual relations within a *gotra* are considered incestuous and are strictly prohibited.

The Extended Family

The size of the family unit is relatively immaterial. In rural areas where the economy is heavily based on agriculture, a family can be quite large and encompass three or four generations, often with everyone living in the same household. Clearly, an agricultural community depends to a much greater degree on an extensive family structure in order to maintain its livelihood and, in hard times, ensure economic and social survival.

In highly urban areas, among more self-sufficient individuals, the family unit might look typically Western, with only the husband, wife and their children under the same roof. These units, because they are smaller, depend to a greater degree on kinship for support. They also have to work harder to maintain those relationships and repay obligations.

This social safety net is there for nearly everyone, even unmarried or widowed persons. Indians understand this but are either unable or unwilling to communicate it to Westerners, who largely do not comprehend the degree with which Indians work to maintain these relationships. Prudent businessmen would be well served to develop an awareness of this phenomenon in their Indian ventures, especially when dealing with older or more traditional Indians.

Strains on the Family Structure

Obviously, even this system is far from perfect. Personality differences, personal greed, and caste tensions lurk beneath the surface at all times. Successful families find ways to deal with these issues. Often it's the patriarch who, as leader of the clan, is called upon to resolve issues. When a resolution to a serious issue cannot be reached, the family may fragment, with a husband taking his wife and children to a new home. In time, this fragment may, itself, grow into a self-sustaining family. Very rarely, however, do the kinship relationships between these two units break down completely.

Life within the family follows clearly defined rules of authority and obedience. This hierarchy is based on age, gender, and blood. Within the ideal patrilineal family, elders are ranked above their juniors, and males are ranked above females of similar age. Wives typically rank below their husband's sisters and below the patriarch's wife. Men are taught to accept responsibility and to lead and manage the unit, while women are taught to maintain a position subservient to the family's needs. Family unity is paramount at all times, although economic growth in the past years has added new pressure to the family structure as young women seek a larger role in the family's economic future.

Ghosts of the Caste

One only needs to look at a sampling of Indian success stories, at home and abroad, to conclude that those Indians not encumbered or oppressed by domestic policies and bureaucracies have enjoyed a distinct advantage over most of their countrymen in business and the professions. Although a self-proclaimed secular state, much of India's social and economic structure is supported on what we in the West have come to know as the caste system (from the Portuguese word *casta*, meaning breed or race). A complex arrangement of social and economic ranking, an individual's caste incorporates elements from their birth (family), skin color, religion, occupation, and language. The magnitude of the caste-derived influence in everyday life is huge: nowhere else on earth can one find an organized socioeconomic structure of this size.

What Is Caste?

Caste is how Westerners understand the traditional segregation of Hindus into broadly defined *Varnas* (meaning colors or arrangement by group, depending on the translator), each of which is a collection of hundreds if not thousands of *Jati*. Translated as "birth," which suggests its ancient roots lie in a hereditary meritocracy, Jati is now widely accepted as an occupationally oriented classification. Within a caste, the Jati, too, are traditionally ranked in a hierarchy. This hierarchy within a hierarchy is further complicated by geography. The relative positions of some Jati within the overall hierarchy change in different parts of the country, although most of the significant differences occur between north and south India.

Similar to traditions in the West, many Indians' family names are based on their Jati. An oft-given example is that of Gandhi, whose name means *greengrocer*. (It should come as no surprise, then, that Mohandas Gandhi belonged to a Vaisia, or trading, caste.) It is their Jati that traditional Indians look to for their most personal identity. For some Indians, their caste is the source of immense personal pride. For others it is penal, a sentence of lifelong oppression.

Evolving Role of Caste

The role of caste in everyday life has been evolving since Independence, when India's new Constitution outlawed caste-based discrimination. However, it is understandably difficult to eradicate thousands of years of ironclad cultural rigidity in just one or two generations.

Historians differ in their opinions about the origin of caste, but it is generally considered to date back thousands of years to the earliest invasions by light-skinned people from regions of southern Europe and Northern Asia (such as Persia, Afghanistan, and Russia). In this theory, these legendary Aryans (from the Sanskrit word *Arya,* which means *good* or *pure*) initiated a social framework that guaranteed and perpetuated their dominion over the Indian subcontinent's darker-skinned native populations. In modern times, "Aryan" has taken on a sinister connotation, one used to justify racial supremacy. The two terms are unrelated as they pertain to Indian culture.

In general terms, there are five principal population divisions resulting from the caste:

1. **Brahmin:** Society's cultural elite, priests, and philosophers/teachers
2. **Kshatria:** Society's aristocrats, rulers, leaders, and warriors/soldiers
3. **Vaisia:** Society's businesspeople, merchants, landlords, and traders
4. **Sudra:** Society's artisans, manual workers, peasants, and laborers in non-polluting jobs
5. **Outcastes:** All those who are not members of the first four divisions

Collectively, these first four groups are sometimes referred to as *clean castes,* because their work does not involve so-called polluting activities.

The Brahmin, Kshatria, and Vaisia are collectively referred to as *high, forward,* or *upper* castes. The high castes account for between 30 percent and 50 percent (depending on the source) of all Hindus and are referred to as "twice born," which reflects their natural birth and their entrance into society (spiritual birth). This spiritual birth occurs at an age between eight and twelve years, depending on the caste. Traditionally and realistically, the high castes have enjoyed economic and social rights and access that have been off-limits for much of the rest of the Indian population. Anyone who is not a member of one of the four castes is an outcaste, the fifth division.

The existence of a Hindu-only caste implies that there also are Indians who live outside its tenets, and indeed this is the case. Westerners need to be aware of the social groups that comprise the traditional caste, as well as the outcastes—Hindu or not—who figuratively lie further down society's ladder.

Untouchables and Other Classes

The outcastes Westerners are most familiar with are the Untouchables, who are Hindu society's classless people laboring in menial, foul, degrading, and dirty jobs often associated with death and waste. This group's name derives from the ancient practice by upper-caste Hindus of rigorously cleansing themselves after any contact with an Untouchable. Their heritage in traditional Indian society is largely that of having virtually no legal status, of social backwardness, and of living in oppressive poverty.

Empowered by the economic and social improvements begun after 1991, more and more of these Indians are referring to themselves as Dalits (from the Hindi meaning *downtrodden, depressed,* or *oppressed*) and are striving hard for their piece of the New India pie. Progress, however, is very slow. According to *National Geographic News,* Dalits represent 90 percent of all impoverished Indians and 95 percent of all illiterate Indians.

As caste is not officially recognized in the Constitution, Central Government population surveys only differentiate the Scheduled Castes and Scheduled Tribes. Dalits are included in the Scheduled Castes, which officially account for 16.2 percent (167 million) of the general population. However, some estimates place their numbers as high as 250 million. Sudras are included in the Backward Classes and are estimated to account for between 35 percent and 50 percent of the population. Upper Castes and Scheduled Tribes make up the balance. The Scheduled Tribes include tribal or native individuals whose remoteness or cultural differences enabled them to escape absorption into the caste hierarchy. Officially, there are 84 million tribal Indians accounting for 8.2 percent of the population. Geographically, the majority of tribal Indians reside in three broad regions: in the Northwest Himalayans near Pakistan and Nepal; in the Northeast Himalayans near Bangladesh, Bhutan, China, and Myanmar; and in the highlands of central India between the Narmada and Godivara Rivers. Smaller groups live in areas west of Bangladesh, southernmost India, and western India.

Attempts at Social Reform

As far back as 150 years ago, there were sustained efforts on the part of enlightened leaders to mitigate the plight of these so-called depressed classes. Under pressure from Indian reformists, the British began taking steps to formally include representation of the depressed classes in their local governments.

In 1935, the Government of India Act established quotas (reservations) for these classes, which were then defined as Scheduled Castes after their tabulation in typically British lists, or schedules. In 1936, the Government of India (Scheduled Castes) Order formalized the schedules of castes throughout India. In 1950, two constitutional orders—the Scheduled Castes Order and Scheduled Tribes Order—formalized and completed the listing of these depressed peoples.

Since Independence, these schedules have been used by the Central Government to develop programs and quotas for the integration and empowerment of all outcastes. The Central Government routinely refers to these Scheduled Classes/Castes, Scheduled Tribes, and (Other) Backward Classes. Collectively, these groups account for a large part of the Indian population.

Discrimination Based on Caste

Discrimination on the basis of caste was officially abolished by the 1950 Constitution but continues today, long after Independence. This discrimination, ranging in form from subtle oppression to outright bloody atrocities, forced the Central Government in 1989 to legislate the Prevention of Atrocities Act, which was intended to guarantee the safety, public health, personal property, educational opportunities, and voting rights of Dalits.

This legislation, while well intentioned, generally served to fan the flames of violence between activist Dalits, as well as other outcastes, and the governing castes. The general Indian population has protested and resisted most attempts by the Central Government to implement legal reservations for the oppressed in jobs, civil service, and schools. Passion for this issue is so deeply ingrained that it brought down the government of then Prime Minister V. P. Singh who, in 1990, sought to implement the decade-old recommendations of the Backward Classes (Mandal) Commission.

Difficulty of Ending Discrimination

Today, this violence between the entrenched clean castes and Scheduled Caste activists continues. This is especially true in rural areas, where Dalits are routinely abused by higher-caste Hindus, despite a 2002 United Nations Resolution that condemned caste and descent-based discrimination. Human Rights Watch routinely addresses caste-based discrimination in its reports, although some critics suggest these reports are disproportionate and bias the reader against significant progress being made in the cities. The majority of outcastes, and violence, occurs at the local and rural level, where the Central Government has little to no control or enforcement capabilities.

A recent example of this can be seen in how aid was distributed along the southeast coast struck by the tsunami in December of 2004. Reports from many impacted regions told of how goods sent to the area were hoarded and distributed according to what can only be described as a caste-based program. Dalit families were widely forced to the rear of food and water lines, tossed out of shelters, denied access to toilet facilities, and made to wait days for first aid and routine medical care. Many private aid groups opted to open separate facilities for the Dalits rather than try to buck the local social and municipal systems. Suffice it to say that most Dalits and tribes received disproportionately little, if any, of the aid.

Caste and caste-based discrimination is not the sole domain of the Hindu community. Many Muslims and Christians live with some form of caste in their everyday lives. Among some groups of Muslims, one social divide exists along the lines of a high caste and a low caste that is analogous to the hierarchy in the Hindu clean caste, that is, between the high castes (Brahmin, Kshatria, and Vaisia) and the Sudra. The other social divide is between these two clean Muslim castes and unclean Muslim Dalits. Among Christians, most of the stigmas associated with caste have disappeared. However, among converts from Hinduism, old ideas die slowly and a subtle but persistent discrimination of (Christian) Dalits by some clergy persists to this day.

For outcastes living in metropolitan areas, especially those cities where economies are booming, the lines between castes tend to blur or even disappear. Here, the historically oppressed have always enjoyed far greater opportunities than their rural brethren. Unfortunately, at the rural level, where the majority of outcaste Indians lives, caste-based prejudice and persecution are still serious matters that threaten to bog down or even derail attempts to introduce social and economic progress. Some pessimists view the tension and violence, resulting from policies intended to improve the status of Dalits, Sudras, and other outcastes, as sufficient to slow or halt the Indian economic miracle and even enough to tear India apart.

Continued Efforts at Social Change

At the national level, India's Central Government is working hard to end this centuries-old feudal system. In 2005, the Central Government saw fit to address similar issues beyond the Dalit communities and proposed legislation to protect the rights of tribal Indians. Further emboldened by this legislation, many Dalits have organized to defend and implement their newfound freedoms. Their uphill battle is going to be a long and bloody one. Unfortunately, these clashes are what is seen on television and read about in newspapers, while the routine discrimination and exploitation continue daily.

The Central Government continues to step up its efforts to enact and enforce legislation creating positive discrimination (what Americans might refer to as affirmative action with quotas) for Scheduled and Backward individuals, in schools and at jobs, in proportion to their presence in the population. Not unexpectedly, this has set off waves of protests at many levels in the country and continues to polarize the Central Government and private-sector interests. Events like this will always make headlines. Sadly, this debate will continue to rage for a long time to come, especially in the less developed areas of the country.

Religion

For well over a thousand years, the Indian subcontinent has concurrently nurtured and sustained two of the world's major, and quite different, religions: Hinduism and Islam. During those thirteen centuries, the relative strength and importance of each has waxed and waned on the fortunes of successive empires, yet both have survived in huge numbers into the twenty-first century. As a result of the August 1947 partition of the country into India and what have become the nations of Pakistan and Bangladesh, Hinduism is by far the most dominant religion in modern India. For every Muslim, there are six Hindus. India also has small populations of Christians, Sikhs, Buddhists, and Jains. Christianity, the world's largest religion but in India only a minor player that accounts for 2.3 percent of the population, came to the subcontinent with the Portuguese and British while Sikhism, Buddhism, and Jainism all originated on the subcontinent.

Sikhism

Compared to the other significant religions of India, Sikhism is a youngster whose 200-year incubation paralleled the major post-Renaissance European colonial excursions to India and the Americas. The religion takes its name from two Sanskrit words that respectively translate as *instruction,* and *discipline* or *learner.* Practiced almost exclusively in the northern state of Punjab, Sikhism's followers subscribe to the teachings of a series of ten gurus who taught in the region between 1507 and 1708. Their legacy is the collection of multilingual scriptures named the Guru Granth Sahib, the so-called *eleventh guru,* whose tenets were drawn from the writings of the ten gurus and other diverse Hindu and Islamic ideas.

Sikhism requires men to cover their heads at all times, so most Westerners recognize practicing male Sikhs by the turban they wear, called a *dastaar.* However, its use is not exclusive to Sikhism, nor do all Sikhs wear it. Sikh nam-

Significant Indian Religions as a Percentage of Population

Religion	Urban	Rural	Nationwide	All Workers	Cultivators
Hindus	82.3	75.6	80.7	83	86.9
Muslims	12.1	17.6	13.6	10	7.1
Christians	2.1	2.9	2.3	2.4	2.2
Sikhs	1.8	1.5	1.5	2.1	1.8
Others	1.7	2.4	1.9	2.5	2

Source: 2001 Census India

ing conventions require men to take the name Singh and women the name Kaur as either their surname or middle name. Unlike Hindus or Indian Muslims, Sikhs do not preclude marriages on the basis of caste. Sikhs comprise approximately 2 percent of the modern Indian population.

Buddhism

Buddhism is less a religion than a philosophy whose origins lie in India but whose glory days there are long gone. Founded on the teachings of Siddhartha Gautama, a fifth-century B.C. nobleman from the north of India, Buddhism spread through the rest of India and into Asia, China, and Japan. Although Buddhism is the world's fifth-largest religion, Buddhists comprise less than 1 percent of the modern Indian population.

Jainism

At the heart of Jainism is a deep respect and concern for all living things and a simple lifestyle that embraces non-violence, vegetarianism, and reincarnation of the soul. A priestless religion without deities, Jainism's roots lie in India's ancient past. An amalgam of philosophy and theology, historians believe its paradigms have played a significant role in the subcontinent's inhabitants' pre-Islamic cultural

Agricultural	Home / Industrial	Other Workers	Non-Workers
85.9	74.6	78.6	78.8
8.9	20.7	14.3	15.2
1.4	1.5	3.3	2.3
1.9	1.8	1.9	1.8
1.9	1.4	1.9	1.9

and spiritual evolution. Today, Jainism's practitioners comprise less than .5 percent of the general population.

Distribution of Religions

Since 1961, the relative overall percentages of individual religions have remained the same. The table on pages 54–55 summarizes the distribution of key religions throughout the Indian population. The inherently strong family and caste structures in India discourage conversion from one religion to another, even though many in the Scheduled Castes have used conversion from Hinduism in an attempt to escape social persecution or create opportunities for advancement.

Racism

Racism in India is a sensitive subject. It's relatively easy for a Westerner to draw parallels between it and caste discrimination. The Central Government insists that the two are separate, unrelated issues, largely on the basis that caste discrimination is illegal under India's Constitution. However, Dalit activists insist they are one and the same because they believe caste discrimination is still a real part of daily life in India. The ancient heroic chronicles of India and Hindu religious stories imply a social hierarchy based on skin color in which lighter-skinned characters and gods routinely triumphed and ruled over darker-skinned characters and devils.

A century ago, cultural anthropologists suggested that the original inhabitants of India, the Dravidians, had been supplanted in the north by the invading Aryans, thus creating a north-to-south cultural and racial orientation. Obviously, Indian soil has seen far more incursions by diverse groups than just the legendary Aryans. The oft-repeated ebb and flow of empires on the subcontinent served to mix the population to some degree. Yet personal sensitivity to skin color is still present, although probably to a lesser degree among educated and young professional Indians in urban areas than in rural areas.

For example, a Brahmin whom I knew very well emigrated from Uttar Pradesh to the United States after finishing college in 1970. Except for a three-year trip home in the late 1970s with his American wife and children, he lived the rest of his adult life here. His skin tone was darker than that of most Northern Indians—more akin to that of someone from Chennai or Sri Lanka—and for the remainder of his life he believed himself somewhat inferior because of it.

Fundamentalism

Occurrences of racism and activism in the name of religion are relatively low in India, despite the huge ideological gaps and relatively violent history between Hindus and Muslims and the recent tensions in the south fomented by Tamil nationalists. At the same time, religious-based tensions between centrist and non-centrist groups inside and outside of government are a real factor in Indian affairs. Since Independence, most high-profile political incidents have been motivated by ideology, such as the assassinations of Mahatma Gandhi by a Hindu fundamentalist, Prime Minister Indira Gandhi by Sikh fundamentalists, and her son and successor, Rajiv Gandhi, by a Tamil fundamentalist.

The friction has been greatest along the edges of the country at its borders with Pakistan and Sri Lanka, where religions and cultures abrade each other with alarming regularity. Occasionally, the heat caused by this friction carries over to other areas of the country, such as the extensive destruction in June 1984 of parts of the Sikhs' holiest religious shrine, the Golden Temple in Amritsar, that led to Indira Ghandi's assassination later that year and subsequently to anti-Sikh riots, or the 1992 destruction of a Muslim shrine in Ayodhya by the Indian Army that spilled over into anti-Muslim rioting by Hindus in Mumbai.

The amount of fundamentalist activities throughout India noticeably increased in the late 1980s and was one of the underlying factors that prompted the initiation of desperately needed economic reforms in 1991. Experts believe that much of the ongoing tension and violence results from festering disputes between very poor or socially deprived groups over shortages of available work, property, or community resources. These conflicts are catalyzed by external incidents into eruptions of political violence along religious lines. Atrocities that take many innocent lives continue to occur, such as the bombing of several commuter trains in Mumbai in 2006.

Gender Attitudes in Indian Society

The economic rewards enjoyed by India's emerging middle class have taken much of the age-old pressures off of young and middle-aged Indian women. Opportunities for professional jobs and employment outside the home have breathed new life into the fight for gender equality. Arranged marriages are becoming rarer as young career-oriented men and women strike out on their own in search of spouses. Dating and matrimony services are a growth industry in all of India's major cities. The odds are good that these are the men and women a *Fortune* 100 U.S. executive will encounter in the boardrooms and executive cafeterias during his or her next trip to India. But is this really the India that executives of most small and medium U.S. companies will be doing business with? Not in the near future, I'm afraid.

Differences in Attitudes

There are significant differences in gender attitudes for people living in urban and rural lifestyles and for people of wealth and status. India's Constitution guarantees equal rights for men and women. This, like some other guaranteed rights, falls short in everyday practice throughout the nation. The United Nations Development Assistance Framework commissioned an independent study, published in 2001, which concluded that women are still generally treated as second-class citizens. The study did not differentiate between women living in poor rural communities and women living in affluent urban areas, although it must be noted that the vast majority of Indian women do live in rural areas and in impoverished conditions. Some of the report's findings are the following:

- Men outnumber women in India, which is the opposite of most countries, because more women than men die before reaching adulthood.
- The majority of girls and women are generally malnourished and in nutritional stress.
- The average Indian woman has little control over her own fertility and reproductive health.
- Female literacy is around 50 percent compared to 66 percent for men, largely because fewer girls have attended school.
- Men far outnumber women in the paid workforce, while women perform the majority of household and pro bono community work.
- Women are generally paid less than men for the same work.
- No woman earns as much as a man in the agricultural sector.
- Women are underrepresented in governance and decision-making positions in ratios ranging from 12:1 to 30:1, respectively.
- Women are legally discriminated against in some land- and property-rights matters.
- Women and women's issues are marginalized in news and news programs, only appearing in 7 percent to 14 percent of all programs and women are usually depicted in traditional female roles.

This is not too surprising. For centuries the social and cultural framework in Indian society has been much kinder to men than it has been to women. Traditional Indian attitudes toward gender are firmly grounded in religion and caste, and they are held to a greater or lesser degree depending on where one lives and how affluent one is. Laws banishing dowry customs and setting minimum ages for marriage (twenty-one for men and eighteen for women) were enacted as recently as 1978.

The Purdah

Many people point toward purdah, the traditional practice in which married women wear veils and seclude themselves, as the root of this bias. Purdah practices are interwoven with other patterns of authority and harmony in the family, and female modesty and decorum are closely tied to family honor. Interestingly, purdah restrictions are greater for traditional women of high-status families, presumably due to the greater need to preserve family honor in the eyes of the community. In traditional communities, personal interaction with the opposite sex is forbidden or highly supervised and American-style dating is nearly unheard of. Purdah is still widely practiced in low-caste rural communities and poor, urban areas. It has largely vanished among educated communities, both rural and urban, although female modesty is still the rule of the day. Among urban and even rural elite women, the practice of wearing veils to cover the face is increasingly considered unsophisticated and even demeaning by some.

Chapter 4

Social Conventions

When living and working in India, it's not unusual to find yourself continually passing back and forth between two worlds: the relatively formal world of Western priorities and protocols, and the seemingly chaotic and richly colorful world of Indian society.

Time

Many Indians experience time differently than Americans do. In the Western world, time is linear. That is, things occur in a relatively logical progression from beginning to end. We are sensitized from birth to the concepts of past, present, and future, and we schedule and conduct our personal and our business affairs accordingly. Anthropologists attribute this sense of linearity to our religious and cultural roots, which are predominantly European.

Traditional Indians, on the other hand, are famous for their relative insensitivity to time. For them, time bends a little to accommodate daily life and their daily routines. Westerners often see themselves as slaves to time. Indians see themselves and the world they live in as integral elements in time. You can see this just about everywhere if you take the time to look for it. Appointments and deadlines are fluid. People move hurriedly or leisurely for reasons that are not apparent to you or me. This has resulted in a society that we might say tolerates enormous inefficiencies.

More recently, the emergence of India onto the global stage has fostered an awareness of the importance that Western companies place on time. In business, for example, successful Indians are becoming increasingly alert to the importance of schedules and deadlines in Western commerce. This does not guarantee that the production superintendent at your Chennai plant is going to start pestering you to install project-control software on the office computer. But it does mean that you can be reasonably confident that the appointment you made with your commercial banker really will take place when scheduled, or at least you'll hear from his office beforehand if he's running late.

The Western (Gregorian) calendar is used in business and just about everything else, except All India Radio broadcasts and official government correspondence. The Indian National Calendar, which is derived from several ancient Hindu calendars, is the official calendar of the government; however, it is not the calendar used to identify holidays. Furthermore, other archaic lunar- and solar-based calendars are still used throughout parts of India, although to a much lesser extent.

You can always tell the calendar in use by how the date is written. For example, December 25, 2008, October 12, 2007, and July 4, 2003 are clearly Gregorian dates, because December, October, and July are Latin months. Chaitra is a Hindu calendar month that overlaps March and April. March 22, 1957, the Gregorian date on which the Indian government adopted the Hindu calendar, is officially 1 Chaitra 1879.

You'll find that people, companies, and cities with experience in dealing with Western businesses are acutely attuned to Western schedules. You should have little difficulty working with Indian businesspeople; just use a little patience and a fair amount of communication.

Fortunately, vacation seasons are fairly regular, with one block beginning in April and lasting through June, when the summer monsoon starts. A second block usually occurs during October after the monsoon. The third block is from mid-December to mid-January.

Business Hours

All work-related hours occur around mid-morning and the afternoon. Exceptions are those cases when people are working with their international counterparts and customers. For example, businesses operating as call centers are active during the overnight hours to coincide with the U.S. business day. Indian Standard Time (centered on New Delhi) is 10.5 hours ahead of Eastern Standard Time in the United States and 5.5 hours ahead of Greenwich Mean Time. India does not use daylight saving time.

Here are some things to keep in mind when considering timing of business:

- **Normal business hours are 9:30 A.M. to 5:30 P.M.** Most offices shut down for lunch between 12:00 and 2:00 P.M. Businesses are open from Monday through Friday, although some are also open on Saturday mornings.
- **Normal government hours are 10:00 A.M. to 1:00 P.M. and 2:00 P.M. to 5:00 P.M.** Government offices are open Monday through Saturday, except on the second Saturday of the month when they are closed.
- **Normal bank hours are 10:00 A.M. to 5:00 P.M. Monday through Friday and 10:00 A.M. to 1:00 P.M. on Saturdays.** Same-day money transactions are not permitted after 2:00 P.M., as opposed to 3:00 P.M. in the United States. ATM machines are appearing all over large cities to help people get cash in a hurry.
- **Normal hours for shops are 10:00 A.M. to 7:30 P.M. Monday through Saturday.** Newer shops in big city malls may keep later or different hours to accommodate the new breed of middle-class shopper.

India's financial year ends in March, so plan your travel and appointments accordingly.

Public Holidays

India is a land of ancient festivals and holidays. Visitors to India have often remarked that there must be at least one holiday being celebrated somewhere in the country every week! Several of the religious holidays mark the beginning or end of periods of observance, such as the Muslim religious observance of Ramadan. For the business traveler, these can interrupt or change normal business activities and patterns for hours, days, and even weeks. Many significant holidays are determined by the Hindu and Islamic calendars, which are based on lunar cycles and regularly change.

India celebrates three national holidays. Eleven other holidays are celebrated along religious lines, and these can vary by region or sect. Collectively, these fourteen holidays are referred to as public holidays. As might be expected, government offices are closed on all public holidays.

The three national holidays are the following:

- **Republic Day: January 26.** On this day in 1950, India's Constitution came into force. Republic Day is celebrated on this date every year.
- **Independence Day: August 15.** In 1947, India gained its independence from Great Britain and became a sovereign nation. Independence Day is celebrated on this date every year.
- **Mahatma Gandhi's Birthday: October 2.** India celebrates the birthday of Mahatma Gandhi, the Father of the Nation who was born in 1869, every year on this day.

The remaining public holidays are celebrated on dates derived from the Hindu calendar and Islamic calendar, which are lunar-based, and the Gregorian calendar. Most are determined from local observations of the phases of the moon. The dates of these holidays change from year to year and may even occur twice in the same (Western) calendar year, as was the case in 2006 for the Muslim festival of Idu'z Zuha/Bakrid. Here is a description of those holidays:

- **Idu'z (pronounced Id-Ul) Zuha/Bakrid:** The Feast of the Sacrifice, this Muslim festival celebrates Ibrahim's test of faith, when Allah ordered him to sacrifice his son, Ismail. Bakrid means sheep and reflects the traditional sacrifice of an animal and subsequent offering of the meat to feed the poor.
- **Muharram:** The first month of the new Islamic year, Muharram is observed on the first day of the Islamic lunar calendar. It is a day of reflection when Muslims commemorate Muhammad's departure from Mecca to live in Medina.
- **Mahavir Jayanthi:** The Jain celebration of the birthday of Vardhamana (*Mahavira* means great hero) in 550 B.C.E. Jains use this day to prayerfully reflect on the principles and founders of the faith.
- **Holi:** Originally a harvest celebration and commemoration of Hindu mythological events, today Holi is a let-loose day of fun that is celebrated on the day after the March full moon.
- **Sri Rama Navami:** This is a quiet day used to celebrate the memory of the incarnated god Sri Rama, Hinduism's ideal man and husband. It falls on the ninth day of the Hindu lunar calendar.
- **Milad-Un-Nabi:** This joyous holiday celebrates the birth of the prophet Muhammad. It occurs around the middle of the third month of the Islamic lunar calendar.
- **Good Friday:** This solemn Christian holy day marks the crucifixion and death of Jesus Christ. Good Friday is the Friday before Easter, which is celebrated on the

Sunday after the first full moon after the spring equinox. Orthodox Christians often observe Good Friday on a different date.

- **Buddha Purnima:** This holiday celebrates the birth of the Buddha.
- **Vijaya Dasami/Dussera:** The culmination of a ten-day festival honoring the divine mother goddess Durga, Vijaya Dasami/Dussera symbolizes new life and is celebrated in the lunar month of Asvina (September–October). Success accompanies new ventures that are started on this day.
- **Eid al-Fitr:** This three-day Islamic festival of gift-giving and celebration of renewal marks the end of the month-long fast of Ramadan. It begins on the first day of the tenth month of the Islamic calendar.
- **Deepavali (Diwali):** This is the much beloved five-day Hindu festival of lights, when families celebrate life and renew kinship and family bonds. It normally occurs eighteen to twenty days after Dussera.

Visitors to certain parts of India will find some differences. For example, in Mumbai you'll officially celebrate the Maharashtrian New Year (Gudi Padwa), Guru Nanak's Birthday, and Christmas Day. You may not officially celebrate Sri Rama Navami or Vijaya Dasami/Dussera.

Business and Social Protocols

As a Westerner, I am constantly on the lookout for specific answers to specific questions, such as how to dress for business meetings, what should and should not be discussed, and so on. But you've read enough here to know that there is no single simple answer to most of these questions. As we know, the vast majority of Indian businesses are family owned and family managed. Some of these businesses are over 150 years old, such as the Tata Group and many small mom-and-pop retailers that have operated out of the same storefronts for generations. Others are brand-new entrepreneurial endeavors started by some fellow just a few years out of college. You're also likely at some point to interact with bureaucrats with a twenty-year tenure in local or Central Government positions. Their professional priorities are markedly different from those of a division manager with Wipro or Infosys.

One key thing to remember is that all these companies and government bureaucracies will somehow reflect the owner's or manager's sense of family values and community culture, which are rooted in their Varna and birthplace. Another thing to remember is that cultures widely differ across the length and breadth of India. Social and cultural protocols in traditional areas of Delhi and Punjab are different from those in Chennai and Bangalore. Despite these differences, the bottom line is that there are a few standard rules to follow. Fortunately, you already know and practice most of them.

It's always to your advantage to find out as much as you can about the culture of the region that you're working in or looking for a venture in, but it's often just not possible. In instances like this, what do you fall back on? Well, unless you're dealing with a company or businessperson getting into his or her first international deal, it's likely that you'll be interacting with seasoned businesspeople already sensitized to the Western style, especially the American style. These people will understand your disorientation and will make the effort to accommodate you during the learning phase. When in doubt, let them take the lead, or at least allow them some room to adjust to your particular way of doing business.

Modern business in India is conducted in much the same way as in the United States. You'll be hard pressed to find a difference between the look and smell of a conference room in Mumbai and one in Los Angeles. Only the refreshments are different.

Professional Protocol and Courtesy

Here are some helpful tips to help American visitors in India stay grounded and take maximum advantage of their time:

- Business intermediaries may or may not be necessary, depending on the business activities you're planning. I highly recommend cultivating relationships with potential intermediaries, such as attorneys, bankers, and government representatives. If you're one of the many Americans who prefers working alone, only you can be the final judge as to their value or necessity.
- The higher up your contacts are in an organization, the better. Everything flows downhill, and you'll get far more respect from a middle manager when your introduction or referral comes from that person's superior.
- Bring a large supply of business cards printed with all your information in English. If you're heading for a specific area or region where you believe adding the local language would be important, you can have the information printed on the reverse side of the card. Remember, though, that it may be difficult to find a competent translator for that language, the font for the language may not exist, some of the information may not translate (or translate correctly) into the foreign language. English is the language of business in India, so the local language shouldn't be necessary. If you're finding that you need it for initial introductions, then you may not be looking in the right place for your first venture.
- Building business and personal relationships is very important. At first, it will seem to you that your Indian counterparts are spending far too much time getting to know you. That's because they really do want to get

to know you. Do whatever you can to establish and develop trustworthiness and credibility with them.

- Indian businesspeople are generally conservative and cautious, by Western standards. New ideas take time to ferment and gel. Don't be offended; this is an issue among Indian corporations, too. The best-known company in India, Tata, has been criticized in the national press for moving too slowly on some business ventures! Remember, too, that many senior and semi-retired Indian executives grew up in the shadow of the British Empire, and they are determined that history will not repeat itself. Give your counterparts as much time and space as you can afford to.

- Professional courtesy is always the rule of the day. First names are not commonly used unless two people are very familiar with each other. In business circles, people address each other as Mr., Mrs., Dr., or by their Indian equivalents. Take your cue from your host. If he addresses you formally, you'll know to do the same when speaking to him or anyone else in the room.

- Women managers and executives are a relatively new phenomenon in India, despite well-publicized stories about highly successful entrepreneurs. Fortunately, women working in the business community are treated with enormous respect, and gender discrimination is rare. It is, however, crucial to your credibility that you sincerely give back that respect to others too.

- Authority usually comes with a touch of gray atop the head. Age and its implied experience are highly respected in India.

- In a group of similar people, you ought to be able to figure out who's in charge because that person will be addressed as "Sir" or "Madam" by everyone else. You may hear someone refer to another colleague at the table as "my brother's good friend" or by another similarly obtuse third-person expression. When this occurs, it's likely that the person being referred to is considered superior to the person speaking. The reference to "my brother" implies a generic older male figure, even though the superior may not be related to the speaker.

- Business dinners are rare. If you go to dinner with business associates, do not expect to discuss business. If business comes up in a discussion, cautiously take advantage of the opportunity and look for cues from your associates as to how deeply they want to pursue it.
- It's not unusual for the negotiation process to morph into a bargaining session. Come prepared to give and take, and you'll both walk away satisfied in the end.

Appropriate Attire

Take a look around your hotel lobby and you'll see people dressed in styles ranging from suits designed last season in Paris to gowns that haven't changed much in 1,000 years. How far can the American businessperson go when indulging a newfound interest in all things Asian? Here are a few suggestions:

- Professional dress is the safest bet for most management and executive-level interactions. Men should wear a suit and necktie. Women should wear slacks or a long skirt with a conservative blouse. Business-casual dress is acceptable at many of the newer companies, but determine ahead of time if this is an option.
- Western women may want to dress in a sari, a salwar suit, or a salwar-kameez. This should be acceptable in most cases, especially in a social setting. Some form of head covering is part of a traditional Indian woman's clothing, so consider ahead of time if this is something you will want to wear. Also, take your cues from your environment. Obviously, you'll feel a bit out of place

if the women in the office you're visiting are dressed in jeans and a blouse.

Interpersonal Relationships

The way you conduct yourself can make the difference between your endeavor's success or failure. Indians are, across the board, a warm and friendly people. Three millennia of working hard to get along with each other have virtually guaranteed this result. Keep in mind that many top Indian business professionals are highly educated, having attended schools modeled on the British private school system. A smaller percentage of these received their advanced education in the United Kingdom. Needless to say, it is likely that you will encounter the stiff upper lip at some point in your work. Don't be offended. Here, in no particular order, are a few basic tips to help you through the day:

- You will see Indians greet each other with their hands held together in a prayer-like position near their hearts and with their heads slightly bowed. This act of greeting is called namaskar. You will also hear the greeting "Namaste," which translates from Sanskrit as "I bow to you." It works; use it.
- English is the language of business, but not everyone you meet will be a businessperson or as fluent in English as you. If you don't understand what someone is saying, politely ask him or her to repeat it. Also, you may have to ask a few questions to determine what's being said. Politely do so, and avoid monopolizing the conversation.
- In all business and social settings, avoid attempting to shake hands with or to touch a woman. If she offers her hand, a polite handshake is acceptable.
- Most Indians are very hospitable and may invite you home for a meal. When your relationship is well established, they may be amenable to your drop-

ping by without an invitation. I recommend that you always call first before doing this.

- Your associates may drop in on you unannounced. Accept them with warmth and grace.
- You are likely to find your Indian counterparts have an enthusiastic curiosity about your personal life and your family. This is a good sign that you are well liked and are being well received. Don't be shy about sharing with them. Also, take the time to ask them about their families.
- Many Westerners are used to getting immediate feedback during conversations and business activities, and find they become frustrated when dealing with their Indian counterparts. As I mentioned earlier, be patient. Traditional Indians are reluctant to say no and can be polite and courteous to a fault.
- I believe that offering sincere compliments and appreciation for the little things people do for you is very important. Argumentative and disagreeable behavior on your part may be considered offensive.
- Most Indians like to converse on a wide range of subjects, especially politics and cricket. It is, however, considered impolite for Westerners to inquire about or discuss religion and sensitive social subjects, like poverty.
- Some of us use our hands when speaking. This is acceptable behavior. Avoid pointing at the person you're talking with, a gesture considered rude, assertive, and intimidating. So is standing with your hands akinbo (on your hips), which also can be interpreted as aggressive and a threat.
- In their own homes, traditional women tend to stay in the kitchen. When they are guests in another's home, traditional women will gravitate to the kitchen.

Food and Drink

There's very little that Americans can do to prepare themselves for an Indian culinary experience. Indian food is highly spiced and flavored. Anthropologists differ on whether this results from the wide availability of the spices or simply their cultural use as food preservatives. Either way, you're in for a real treat.

Indian food in the United States does not taste quite the same as a freshly prepared meal in India. Basic ingredients are often different or unavailable. Cookware and ovens are made from different materials and are heated by different fuels. It should come as no surprise that food across India varies as widely as language and culture. Thus, it's difficult to offer a universal list of must-try dishes. Perhaps it's safest to know that the most famous Indian cuisine, tandoori dishes (those cooked in a clay oven), are endemic to the far north around Delhi and even the Punjab, while kebobs are usually associated with Muslim cooking found in areas near Pakistan and Bangladesh.

Like food in other foreign, subtropical, and tropical regions of the world, Indian food, especially its microbiology, is different from American fare. It may take a little while for your system to adjust to meals like salads or to uncooked appetizers. This isn't unusual; Indians traveling in the United States often have the same problem with our food. For example, a very good friend of mine steers toward Mexican restaurants when having to eat out during his infrequent visits to the United States.

Try to avoid uncooked food or food from street vendors. Hepatitis is a much bigger health problem in India than it is in the United States, and the U.S. Centers for Disease Control recommends travelers be vaccinated against hepatitis A, hepatitis B, and typhoid. When dining in India, there are just a few basic rules to follow and things to remember:

- Hindus, especially those in the higher, clean castes, generally don't eat meat, and they shun beef. However, don't be surprised if one of your less-traditional Hindu associates orders a sizzling buffalo steak the next time you're at dinner in a Western-style restaurant.
- Muslims generally don't eat pork, and they usually don't drink alcohol.
- Vegetarians can avoid meat relatively easily, especially on short trips and even in Western-style restaurants, by sticking with lentil-bean–based meals called *dals*. The majority of Indian vegetables are like those in the United States. They appear in markets seasonally (like they used to here in the States before we started importing vegetables from warmer climates year round). Due to this, vegetarian menus change a great deal with the seasons.
- Lean, fresh goat is the staple meat used in most non-vegetarian Indian meals. Its taste is unmistakable. Restaurant menus may offer mutton, but don't expect this to be from a lamb or a sheep. Goat served in India is tougher than Western meats, so Indians in America often slow-cook their very lean lamb in lots of oil to try and get that home-cooked taste. If you're planning to eat meat dishes while in India, I recommend you frequent your local Indian restaurants here in the United States beforehand and see if they can prepare you a variety of dishes as closely as possible to what they serve in their own homes. Tell them in advance of your upcoming trip, and they'll be eager to help you.
- Many Indians use their right hand to eat their meals. Soft, flat naan bread (brought to India by Hindus from the Pakistan/Afghanistan border after Partition) and pooris are served in an Indian restaurant for scooping and eating food. There's even a north-south bias

in this; Northern Indians usually use their fingertips while Southern Indians may plunge their entire hands into the food. Don't fret; it's perfectly acceptable for you to stick with your knife and fork.

- Hot and spicy food used to be more of a regional phenomenon but is becoming more and more widespread. The heat in Indian cooking comes from chili peppers, which are often cooked whole in the meal. Locating and carefully removing the peppers before ravenously digging in can help you avoid an unplanned, unpleasant experience.
- You may see the term *garam masala* on a menu. Although it means "hot spices," it actually refers to a wonderful blend of flavors that warms the body but doesn't burn the tongue.
- Better Indian restaurants tend to not ask if you'd like your food mild, medium, or spicy because the heat is usually cooked into the dish when it's prepared as opposed to being added afterwards. Be prepared to wait longer for a dish that you want prepared differently from how it's intended; a good chef does all things from scratch. Ask your host/guest or the waiter/chef to recommend something that fits your tastes.
- Business lunches are becoming more and more commonplace. Many urban restaurants have light fare and less-spicy menus that appeal to Westerners and will make seating arrangements to accommodate groups of four or more. Calling ahead for reservations is recommended for larger groups.
- When all else fails and you can't avoid a scorching meal, stick with very small portions.

Travel, Money, and Numbers

Even today, traveling to and within India presents a few special challenges. As in other developing countries, getting around and paying your bills in India requires a little advanced planning and some reorientation to a different money system and numerical convention.

Travel

Business travel to and in India is rapidly becoming more and more sophisticated. Top U.S. executives are ferried back and forth on private jets and helicopters. However, getting around once back on the ground can be a bit of an adventure, especially if you insist on taking the wheel yourself. For this reason, as well as a host of others, I strongly recommend that you prearrange all your travel through a reputable business travel agent. Legacy providers, such as American Express and Thomas Cook, can handle all your entry visa arrangements and help you through unforeseen crises with their small business and corporate travel services. I recommend you get in touch with them right away. It's often better than having your own in-house travel department.

Beyond the need to handle business-related travel issues, most good travel guides should be sufficient to help you enjoy your stay and even do some exploring.

Money

The Indian rupee is equally divided into 100 paise. Inversely, a paisa is 100th of a rupee.

Paper money is available in 10-, 20-, 50-, 100-, 500-, and 1,000-rupee notes. You also are likely to see 5-rupee notes. These are legal but no longer printed. Coins are available in the amount of 25 and 50 paise, and 1, 2, and 5 rupees.

Rupees and dollars are fully convertible. The exchange rate has been fairly stable, but is slowly changing in favor of the rupee.

Exchanging dollars for rupees requires a little paperwork, especially in larger cities and travel centers like airports where crowds are large. Importing and exporting rupees into and out of India is illegal. When leaving India, plan to change your rupees back to dollars at a bank or reputable money-changer (such as American Express, Thomas Cook, or Cox & Kings) before heading to the airport.

The standard solution to money management is to use major credit cards, such as Visa, MasterCard, and American Express. Diners Club is also accepted in some places. ATM machines are popping up everywhere in the big cities, but check with your bank to be sure your card will work.

Numbers

Indians use the same Arabic numerals used in the West. However, there are differences in the names and depictions of very large numbers: in the Indian system, numbers are punctuated every two places rather than every three places. Here are the keys to help you avoid a costly mistake:

- Up to 99,999 the numbers are written and spoken the same as they are in the West.
- 100,000 = 1 lakh, written as 1,00,000 (same number of zeroes as 100,000, but with an additional comma after the leading 1).
- 1,000,000 = 10 lakh and is written 10,00,000.
- 10,000,000 = 100 lakh = 1 crore and is written 1,00,00,000.
- 100,000,000 = 10 crore and is written 10,00,00,000.
- 1,000,000,000 = 100 crore and is written 1,00,00,00,000.

If you're not sure about the number you're looking at, ask someone for help. And remember that average Indians may struggle with U.S. numbers, too.

Chapter 5

Market-Success Factors

India's uniqueness goes far, far deeper than the surface we see. Much of India's success in the information technology (IT) and business process outsourcing (BPO) fields had to do with the surplus of a significant number of educated young people. The resource was there, and all that was needed was to identify the means to tap into it.

What other human resources does India have on tap for the Western entrepreneur? Well, we already know that most of the sectors that employ India's best and brightest are running into difficulty finding well-qualified candidates. Many of these workers are finding out that their country is such a hot commodity that they can strike out on their own as entrepreneurs and do very well.

This bodes well for the U.S. businessperson looking for opportunities with Indian entrepreneurs. But what does it say about the Midwestern manufacturing company looking to set up shop somewhere on the subcontinent? What strategic human-resource factors must this firm consider to ensure its success? Have any U.S. companies encountered so much difficulty establishing an Indian operation that they retrenched or entirely pulled out of the country? (I can think of a few—can you?)

This chapter reviews and discusses the strategic factors and associated risks that I believe are among the most important for the U.S. businessperson to consider and thoroughly understand before consummating any deal. Regardless of the perceived opportunities, the facts of daily life will ultimately determine the success of your operation. For example, you may find it necessary to include worker training and skills development, language improvement classes, and other similar resource-building measures into your operation. Or safe transportation for your female employees and contractors may be the order of the day if your operation is located in an unsavory part of town. I highly encourage you to consider these details, as a small investment will reap enormous rewards in terms of employee loyalty and improved performance. As you'll see, business success in India requires more than just counting the beans.

Languages

The language system of India and Southeast Asia is a fascinating subject worthy of the many scholarly books that have been written about it. Needless to say, I'll confine myself to discussing the role of language in everyday life and what that means to your ability to get business done. You should expect an educated, middle-class Indian businessperson to speak at least two if not three languages, in this order: the predominant language of his or her home state or territory, Hindi, and English. If the person isn't fluent in Hindi and English, you may want to rethink that particular relationship.

For most highly educated Indians, English should come as naturally as their first language, which is the language they think in and often the first language they learned as a child. On the other hand, the average Indian speaks an English that is somewhat different from American English.

Most English-speaking Indians struggle with many formalities of the English language and are somewhat unfamiliar with many contemporary U.S. slang and idiomatic expressions. Their English has been shaped and trimmed to fit their culture and their own languages. The net result of this has been the creation of words and expressions that have different meanings or that you may never have heard before or anywhere else.

For example, Indian penal codes talk about the illegality of *eve teasing,* which is a catchall term for the sexual harassment of women. Newsletters about international affairs refer to *Pak,* which is an abbreviation for Pakistan or Pakistani. It is a good idea to err on the side of caution. It's not a good idea to presume that your Indian partner or agent knows what you're talking about all the time. Always take the time to confirm that you understand what someone is telling you.

India's twenty-eight states and seven union territories were proudly carved out on the basis of language. Over 25 percent of all Indians (300 million) live in urban areas—that is, in one of India's fifty-one cities, 384 urban agglomerates, or 5,161 towns. The remaining 74 percent (around 810 million people) live in rural areas and small towns, many with their own language variants. The English language is virtually unknown among the poorer residents in rural areas. It might only be spoken by a few of the more educated elite or local administrators, and probably not that well.

In trying to distance itself from its English colonial past, the framers of India's Constitution used hopeful language that named Hindi as the country's official tongue and restricted the use of English in official circles. Although English is the lingua franca of business, India's current language policy perpetuates some confusion. It simultaneously attempts to develop more uniformity in native languages and to perpetuate language traditions.

Today, the Indian government recognizes twenty-two major languages—Sanskrit and twenty-one modern variants of regional languages. Marginalized by India's Constitution, English is not recognized as one of these official languages. These are not curiosities or slang versions of Hindi but are distinct languages falling into two general families: Indo-Aryan, which is spoken by about three-quarters of the population and is dominant in the northern parts of the country, and the so-called Dravidian, which is spoken by about one-quarter of the population in the southern parts of the country. The remaining 2 percent of the population, living mostly in the northeast and northwest, speak languages with ancient Austric and Tibeto-Burman roots. Hindi, which is spoken by over half of the population, is the single best-known language. Its forty-nine varieties constitute the predominant languages in six Indian states and minor languages in seven other states.

Languages Other Than English and Hindi

That was the easy part. Now, are you ready for this? Besides the twenty-two officially recognized languages, the Indian census acknowledges well over 1,500 distinguishable languages and other so-called mother tongues—languages supposedly spoken by one's mother. There are 574 recognized Indo-Aryan languages and 153 recognized Dravidian languages that constitute about one-third and one-fourth, respectively, of all recognized Indian languages.

There are an estimated twenty-five writing systems, of which fourteen are considered major systems. Of these fourteen, twelve are derived from the ancient Brahmin script. On a routine daily commute somewhere in the country, an average Indian can go to the local newsstand and theoretically buy a copy of one of over 5,500 daily newspapers and one of nearly 350 weekly newsmagazines regularly published in nearly 100 languages. Radio programs are broadcast in at least twenty languages and nearly 150 dialects. Films are released in as many as fifteen languages, including French and Portuguese.

Indian multilingualism has evolved in two ways: naturally, as languages are spoken every day through the population, and through schooling, where between fifty to seventy languages are either taught or studied. The official government policy is to help all languages develop into fit vehicles of communication in their designated areas of use. This policy accommodates everyday quirks and is ever-evolving. India's Department of Higher Education encourages the use of mother tongues in certain situations while accommodating differences and allowing language evolution through mutual adjustment, consensus, and the judiciary.

Functional Illiteracy

From a business perspective, literacy rates are important in determining the workforce's location, gender, and age. Like language, literacy in India also is a moving target. Official government statistics proudly and rightfully point to an outstanding increase in the national literacy since Independence—from 18 percent in 1951 to 65 percent in 2001. This is remarkable progress by any measure, despite the nearly overwhelming forces of cultural differences, lack of resources, and explosive population growth.

The single largest jump in literacy was in the decade between the 1991 and 2001 censuses, when the official literacy rate increased from 52 to 65 percent. The 2006 United Nations Human Development Report published an adult literacy rate of 60 percent—70 percent for men and 48 percent for women—for persons aged fifteen and older.

In general, the literacy rate is much higher in urban areas than it is in rural areas. The Indian government has published the following figures, which curiously don't yield 65 percent.

Urban-Rural Gaps in Literacy (In Millions of Persons)

	Men	Women	Total
Urban	113.6	86.4	200
Rural	226.3	140.4	366.7
Total	339.9	226.8	566.7

Source: India Census 2001, as published by the Department of Higher Education

In order of decreasing literacy rate, here is how the states and union territories were ranked by the 2001 census:

- **High literacy (above 80 percent):** Kerala, Mizoram, Lakshadweep, Goa, Delhi, Chandigarh, Pondicherry, A and N Islands, and Daman and Diu
- **Above-average literacy (65 to 80 percent):** Maharashtra, Himachal Pradesh, Tripura, Tamil Nadu, Uttaranchal, Gujarat, Punjab, Sikkim, West Bengal, Manipur, Haryana, Nagaland, and Karnataka
- **Below-average literacy (below 65 percent):** Chhattisgarh, Assam, Madhya Pradesh, Orissa, Meghalaya, Andhra Pradesh, Rajasthan, Dadra and Nagar Haveli, Uttar Pradesh, Arunachal Pradesh, Jammu and Kashmir, Jharkland, and Bihar

Of the nine highly literate states and territories, only Kerala was ranked above 90 percent literacy with a rate of 90.9 percent.

On a state-by-state basis, literacy generally correlates with wealth. Exceptions do occur however. For example, Punjab is India's wealthiest state as determined by per-capita income, but its literacy rate is only a few points above the national average.

Obviously, literacy rates must also be viewed in terms of a person's primary language. Tamil speakers, for example, cannot be validly tested for literacy in another state's language that they don't know, no matter how glib or intelligent they may be. Thus, the government's recognition of twenty-two major languages has the net effect of diluting the national average rate for literacy, because there are clearly less people capable of speaking the languages in demand by the business community, namely English and Hindi. In such instances, useable average literacy rates might drop to 25 percent of the country's population, or less.

What Is Literacy?

By now I hope your curiosity has been aroused enough to ask, "What is literacy?" Unlike here in the United States, India has had difficulty answering this question. Here are some definitions and criteria that have been used by various authorities in India:

- The United Nations defines basic literacy as the ability to read forty words per minute, write twenty words per minute, and perform two-digit arithmetic. Thus, literacy rates reported by the UN are likely to be based on this definition and lower than those reported by official Indian agencies that use less-stringent definitions.
- India's National Literacy Mission defines literacy as ". . . basic literacy and numeracy skills, functional knowledge useable in day-to-day affairs and social awareness." This is a political definition that counts "common sense and life experience" as a component of literacy to include the huge number of adults that have never attended school.
- The Indian government's census data cites literacy and illiteracy rates as they pertain to persons in the "7+ age group," which is the U.S. equivalent of a first-grade education. This is a key point for businesspeople to realize: that literacy rates in India could mean the "literate" Indian worker you hire may be no more literate than an average U.S. first-grader.

Regardless of the way it's been defined, contemporary Indian thinking on literacy includes people's ability to function within their community and to have the problem-solving skills necessary to make critical life-related decisions. However, lumping a person's knowledge, awareness, and their sensitivity to income inequality, racial and religious persecution, and gender bias in with literacy is risky and clouds the fundamental issue.

Trends for the Near Future

Since Independence, India has crafted several national programs to improve the literacy rate, and expenditures on overall public education are nearly 3 percent of GDP. However, expenditures on promoting literacy are low, and most of the programs have been shut down, matured and retired, or migrated to passive media (such as using subtitles on television programs to teach language skills). Instead, much of the government's effort is focused on educating children in schools.

This suggests that a portion of the population that missed out on school opportunities may remain illiterate for the rest of their lives. Access to adequate education is becoming an important issue among India's urban and rural poor, who see the disparity between themselves and the emerging urban middle class as an ever-widening chasm that will have to be bridged one way or another. The Central Government also realizes that simple set-asides of government seats and university admissions are only stopgap measures that fail to address the fundamental issue of education.

Income Inequality

The Indian government isn't saying it very loudly, but its single biggest social commitment is to close the gap between the country's haves and its have-nots. Lessons have been learned by taking a hard look at other countries with similar demographics, like modern Brazil and eighteenth-century France, and remembering how social inequity affected economic and political stability. More recently in 1997, fallout from the Asian flu was deeply felt in the economies of many developing countries.

Whether the problems are real or just perceived, what is it that India's leaders are concerned about? Here are some facts to consider:

- 80 percent of all Indians lives on less than $2 per day, and 34 percent lives on less than $1 per day.
- Just about half of the world's poorest people live on the Indian subcontinent: 41 percent in India, 3.9 percent in Pakistan, and 3.5 percent in Bangladesh.

- China, one of India's former sparring partners and likely a future economic partner, is next in line, with 22 percent of the world's poorest people. The entire continent of Africa is third, with about 20 percent of the world's poor.

My reason for pointing this out isn't to elicit an emotional response from you, the reader, and I'm certainly not passing the hat on anyone's behalf. Rather, "no surprises" is the order of the day here.

How Wide Is the Gap?

So far, much of the Indian miracle has benefited a fraction of the population, while the rest have continued to live extraordinarily marginal lives. We've already discussed some of the factors that contribute to this, such as social conventions, language barriers, and lack of education. But simply alluding to some statistics about numbers of people and their incomes does little to frame what ought to be addressed by business and the government to ensure the miracle continues.

How can income inequality be defined? "With difficulty," is the answer. All of the standard or accepted measures compare incomes of the richest people to incomes of the poorest people or look at various components of a country's social safety net. Those yardsticks do not work for India because her enormous population skews the results toward the average Indian, who is very poor to begin with.

For example, contemporary measures of inequality place India, Pakistan, and Bangladesh on par with Russia, Canada, and much of Western Europe. These same metrics show Indians are more equal than citizens of the United States, China, and Australia and far better off than most residents of Latin America and southern Africa. Instead of using those measures of comparison, I believe it is important to view India's income disparity in two parts: urban and rural.

Opportunity Starts in Urban Areas

The astute U.S. investor isn't the only one following the money trail to India's biggest cities. The populations of India's major cities have more than quadrupled since Independence, and about half of that growth is attributed to immigration from rural areas. With the completion of the national highway system (the Golden Quadrilateral), more and more Indians will be able to travel in search of opportunities in areas that their fathers could only dream of seeing.

India's major cities are where you will find the highest socioeconomic groups thriving—working in office towers, living inside walled compounds, and traveling the world on luxury jets. Overall living conditions range from excellent for the well educated and well connected to deplorable for the poorest immigrants. Kinship systems structured along caste or place of origin attempt to tide newcomers over until they are able to assimilate into the local economy. Jobs in labor and cleaning for the poorest, when those jobs can be found, are typically the norm for those from the lowest castes and the uneducated. The more entrepreneurial open stands and hawk all sorts of homemade utensils and goods, such as hand-woven baskets and oven-fired clay products.

India's emerging middle class would not exist without the opportunities that the big cities offer. The most publicized sectors have been IT and BPO services, but the boom of the cities goes far beyond those two. Construction of housing and commercial space creates opportunities for laborers, managers, and investors. Couples, families, and businesses moving into these new spaces create previously unknown opportunities for services, retailers, and a host of other support activities. People who previously walked are starting to ride bicycles. Former bicycle riders are now on motorized scooters purchased from individuals who have moved on to small cars. Office workers travel in carpools or use car services started by entrepreneurs.

The Need for Manufacturing

But cities like Mumbai, Bangalore, and Delhi may not be the best places for country people to migrate into. These cities and others riding the high-tech and business waves cater to the professional elite and the young urban middle class. Formal jobs for the majority of India's poor and marginalized just aren't there. Instead, the country's manufacturing centers must step up to the plate and create these opportunities. Cities like Surat and Ahmadabad are where the future lies for much of India's poor.

Can this happen? Yes, it can, but it's still a long way off. Much of the government's rhetoric about economic growth whitewashes the need to jump-start the country's manufacturing base and expand it into rural areas. Right now hundreds of thousands of poorer people commute for hours every day into and out of the cities. Wages are extremely low, by urban standards, but jobs are still better than what can be had through farming or herding. Those with some education are finding clerical and low-level supervisory jobs that pay better and afford them the opportunity to send their children to private elementary schools, where they'll get an education that should better prepare them for college. To support this sector, India desperately needs to improve its balance of trade in favor of exports.

Opportunities in Rural Areas

As long as India's economic miracle continues, there's little chance that anyone will intentionally upset the apple cart. Should a significant slowdown occur, the interface between the urban haves and have-nots might start to rub a little raw. Prudent people with some personal savings should be able to withstand normal setbacks. The urban poor, who have precious little, may be forced back to their rural roots. This will be difficult for them, because they have tasted the fruit of a better life and will see any steps backwards as utterly unfair—

and perceived unfairness is one of the most basic causes of human tension and triggers for social unrest.

Out in the countryside, life for most of India's population goes on relatively unchanged. This is where the greatest relative imbalances occur and where most of the 800–odd million living on less than $2 per day toil in anonymity. In the near term, the power of ancient social and economic standards will ensure that the status quo is observed. But, in the years to come, more and more of the poor and the subjugated will begin looking for their place in the sun. Ambitions fanned by tales of skyscrapers and luxury cars, gleaming shops, and raucous discos may foster ill-will, and revenge that will not go unquenched.

Gender Bias in Everyday Business

Gender bias is gradually disappearing among the middle and upper classes of Indian society. The demand for qualified workers and the creation of entrepreneurial opportunities has benefited women as well as men. Major newspapers and magazines publish stories about successful wives who create their own careers using their own merits and capabilities while their spouses don the househusband mantle. In families in which both spouses work, the grandparents take care of the household. If the grandparents are not available, child care and hired help are becoming the norm.

But it's not like this everywhere in the country, or even in the city. Old social stigmas and the lack of education for women continue to take a bite out of the Indian economy. The fact that many of India's poor and uneducated women are treated unfairly is no secret. It's in the language, it's in the classical literature, and it's in the caste. This acknowledgment is not intended to disparage India's rich and varied history or to look differently at the personal and professional accomplishments of many Indian women, but to understand how male-centric social behavior affects all ranks of working women in everyday life.

Rural women and men who come to the cities to work are paid different wages, with the man receiving more. Why? Well, for example, many young women bring their children with them to work and have to take time out of their day to care for or nurse them. Employers often use this as an excuse to pay less for the perceived fewer hours that the women work. Also, some women are unmarried or self-employed. An enlightened Westerner would quickly scoff at this male-oriented behavior and push for equality. Will this work in India? How important is being male in India and how strongly does this importance influence a person's behavior throughout his or her life?

The Roots of Gender Bias

Sociologists point toward several factors that contribute to gender bias in India. In a research paper focused on measuring gender bias, Diganta Mukhergee of the Indian Statistical Institute in Kolkata pointed out that religion, family size, and the mother's level of education were strong factors in sustaining the bias toward having male children in the rural population data that was studied, and that this bias was present in a large proportion of the general population.

P. Arokiasamy and Jalandhar Pradhan of the International Institute for Population Sciences in Mumbai reviewed data to determine if gender bias was a regional phenomenon. They concluded that there is a significant degree of gender bias against female children in most north and north-central Indian states. Data for immunizations against disease and attendance in school suggest a systematic neglect of girls throughout the country. The exceptions are Maharashtra, where gender bias seems marginal, and Kerala, where conditions for girls are favorable. (It should be noted that Kerala is the only Indian state where adult literacy is over 90 percent.) Clearly, then, boys are generally favored even before birth and the message sent to the girls has been that they are on their own or destined to finish second.

Self-Employed Women's Association (SEWA)

If there's going to be a social revolution in favor of poor women, it will have to start in the cities—and it already has. One of the best examples of this has been going on in the workplace for over thirty years. Since 1972, the Self-Employed Women's Association (SEWA) has been assisting nearly 750,000 of India's poor women, many in the city of Ahmedabad. Its roots go back to 1917, when Mahatma Gandhi led a successful labor strike of textile workers that inspired the founding in 1920 of the Textile Labor Association for India's mill workers. In 1954, the Textile Labor Association founded its Women's Wing to provide training and welfare services to the wives, daughters, and widows of its mill-worker members. In the late 1960s, a wide range of classes in sewing, knitting, embroidery, spinning, typing, and stenography were introduced. As more and more abuses of women workers came to light, the Textile Labor Association found itself working harder on behalf of homeless and underpaid women workers; a natural evolution to the formation of the SEWA as India's first trade union without identifiable employers followed in 1972.

During the 1980s, a rift occurred between SEWA and the Textile Labor Association. When the Central Government began its policy of reserving jobs for Dalits and Scheduled Tribes, higher castes began to attack Dalits, and severe rioting broke out in many of India's cities. The SEWA took an outspoken, supportive position for its members, many of whom were victims of the riots. However, the Textile Labor Association chose to remain quietly on the sidelines and subsequently broke ranks with the SEWA. Following this schism, and freed from the reins of the caste-oriented Textile Labor Association, SEWA membership quickly grew, and its influence began to expand from Ahmedabad into rural areas.

Today, SEWA is highly reflective of India's Unorganized Sector, where 94 percent of the country's women work as laborers, hawk goods as street vendors, or work at semi-skilled crafts like weaving, washing, cleaning, and cooking. SEWA is dedicated to empowering its members by offering services and training that will enable them to devote more time to earning a living and ultimately to become self-reliant. Some services, such as child care, are fee-based. But these fees help maintain a mutually supportive environment for the members. Midwives, too, are members of SEWA.

SEWA recognizes that India's emergence as an economic power on the global stage means changes for its members. On the one hand, economic growth means new opportunities will present themselves. On the other, it also means that wages may start lagging behind those of other women in society as new jobs go to skilled and semi-skilled workers, as production of home-grown products is taken up by small businesses eager to enter the export economy, and as competition for their own jobs increases as workers from other parts of the country migrate toward and into India's historic manufacturing centers. Issues that SEWA has tackled include the following:

- Clean Ahmedabad Campaign
- Construction Workers' Campaign
- Food Security Campaign
- Forest Workers' Campaign
- Home-Based Workers' Campaign
- Minimum Wages Campaign
- The Recognition of Midwives Campaign
- The Recognition of Unorganized Sector Workers Campaign
- The Right to Child Care Campaign
- (Street) Vendors' Campaign
- The Water Campaign

Some have met with more success than others, but all are sincere efforts that have generated international visibility.

Crime and Personal Security

India's major cities are among the most crowded places in the world, with population densities that would make a native New Yorker cringe. Squeeze enough people, vehicles, and animals into one place, and things are going to happen, right? Well, remarkably, no.

Based on information provided by the U.S. State Department's Bureau of Consular Affairs and India's National Crime Records Bureau, if you keep your wits about you, India is a remarkably safe place to be. It's not perfect, but then again, nowhere is. The other thing that you must remember at all times is that while in India, you are subject to all its laws and regulations. Actions and expressions used every day in the United States may be unacceptable or even illegal in India. This is especially true when dealing with business–women because Indian society's treatment of women is far more conservative than that of American society. You can and will go to jail if you violate certain protocols of behavior.

U.S. State Department Recommendations

The probability of becoming a crime victim is somewhat different for tourists than it is for businesspeople, although there are places and activities, such as when traveling cross-country in politically active areas, where risks are present for both. In general, it is recommended that Americans—and especially women—not travel alone along the border between India and Pakistan, anywhere in Jammu and Kashmir, and in tribal areas of the far northeast, east central, and south, where Naxalite groups (described on page 110) may be present or active. Although India has seen its share of terrorist violence in which a few Americans have been injured or killed, it appears that these victims were simply in the wrong place at the wrong time and were not the intended targets. Much of the terrorist activity is either religious or political in nature and has taken the form of isolated car and train bombings. The U.S. State Department does point out that anti-American groups are suspected of being in India, but they have made no claims. In 2006, a false alarm occurred in Goa when rumors spread among American tourists and students about a possible al-Qaeda attack, which never occurred.

According to the U.S. State Department, which takes a cautious view toward overseas travel, Americans are more likely to become victims of petty crimes and inadvertently injured, or worse, by the following:

- Swimming in strong, open-water currents along the Indian coastline
- Being caught up in a street demonstration or a large, unruly holiday crowd
- Riding trains or buses alone or at night
- Traveling alone by taxicab to and from major airports
- Displaying money
- Driving in a large city
- Getting involved with a scam artist

Americans involved in social and religious activities, such as handing out political or religious literature, preaching, or working with Indian authorities, have been attacked and injured. Most of these incidents have occurred outside rather than in large cities.

Businesses and businesspeople have rarely been the targets of violence or crime, although Naxalites in tribal states and gangs in large cities have attacked symbolic targets like American companies, blackmailed American organizations, possibly set off a small bomb as part of a suspected extortion plot, and targeted unsuspecting businesspeople for possible kidnap and ransom. Foreigners have been robbed while in taxicabs going to and from Mumbai's airports, and police suspect the drivers were complicit in the robberies. Pickpocketing of personal effects and U.S. passports seems to be the crime that occurs the most often.

The U.S. State Department makes special mention of corruption-related crimes against U.S. businesspeople that we haven't seen in this country in 100 years. For example, Indian law allows the police to arrest anyone accused of committing a crime, no matter how frivolous. Unscrupulous or dissatisfied Indian businessmen sometimes take advantage of this quirk in the legal system and have been known to escalate civil or personal disagreements into criminal charges. Americans have reportedly been jailed for surprisingly long periods of time until the matters were resolved.

Also, salespeople traveling with samples of professional equipment, commercial supplies, and goods for trade fairs and exhibitions are encouraged to use so-called merchandise passports, or carnets, to avoid paying import duties and taxes on items they'll be taking back or re-exporting from India within one year. ATA (Admission Temporaire – Temporary Admission Carnets) can be obtained from the United States Council for International Business for use in sixty-nine countries, including India, to safely and smoothly move these items through customs.

India's National Crime Record

India's National Crime Records Bureau publishes data and statistics reported to it by the states and union territories. It's worthwhile to have some understanding of the Indian criminal codes and types of crimes so that you can take the appropriate actions if something distasteful happens to you or to a business colleague. You also can use data published by the bureau to help select (or avoid) a location for your business.

Under India's Criminal Procedure Code, all crimes fall into one of two categories:

1. Cognizable crimes are those in which the police can make an arrest, without a warrant, when they receive a complaint or find evidence of a crime. The previous

example of the businessman frivolously accused of a crime by a disgruntled associate would be a typical chain of events for a cognizable crime.

2. Non-cognizable crimes are those where the police have no authority to make an arrest without a warrant or magisterial permission. Parties affected by non-cognizable crimes are usually required to seek recourse in the courts.

Cognizable crimes broadly fall into one of two categories: those under the Indian Penal Code (IPC) or those under Special or Local Laws (SLL). The IPC is analogous to U.S. federal law, and SLL is analogous to state law. Here are some examples of each:

- **Crimes under the IPC:** Murder, kidnapping, robbery, burglary, theft, rioting and arson, criminal breach of trust, counterfeiting, cheating, rape, dowry death, molestation, sexual harassment of girls, and crimes against children including kidnapping, selling/buying for prostitution, child rape, and abandonment
- **Crimes under the SLL:** Cyber law, narcotics, gambling, immoral traffic, passport and visa registration, antiquities and art treasures, indecent representation of women, and copyright infringement

In 2004, which is the most recent year for which complete data have been available, the nationwide cognizable crime rate (IPC and SLL) was slightly above 0.5 percent (555.3 reported crimes per 100,000 persons) and was higher than in all previous years.

Urban Crime

In some of India's biggest cities, which is where you are likeliest to be setting up your operation, problems such as unchecked migration, illegal settlements, social and cultural disparities, and unequal incomes are causing crime rates to climb at record levels. Also, organized groups, gangs, professional criminals, and juveniles are finding crime to be the quickest way to a more lavish lifestyle. Here are some facts worth considering:

- The IPC crime rate in India's largest urban agglomeration centers was 70 percent higher than the national average—287.3 per 100,000 in the cities versus 168.8 per 100,000 nationwide. Crime rates in these cities were higher than in the respective states where they're located. Delhi, Mumbai, and Bangalore reported increases of 15.7, 9.5, and 9.2 percent, respectively, in IPC crimes. Topping the list was Agra (home of the Mughal Emperor Shah Jahan's crown jewel, the Taj Mahal, and India's second most-popular tourist destination), which reported an increase of 54.6 percent in IPC crimes.
- The SLL crime rate in these same cities was 450 percent higher than the national average—1,743.5 per 100,000 in the thirty-five largest cities versus 386.6 per 100,000 nationwide. Kolkata topped the list with a rate of nearly 10 percent—9,624.1 per 100,000 persons!

In total, India's largest cities reported an average total crime rate (IPC plus SSL) of 2,030.8 per 100,000.

How does this compare to the United States? Well, in 2004 New York City was the country's safest big city, with an overall crime rate of 2,800 per 100,000, making it 37 percent less safe than the average Indian big city. With a crime rate of 8,959 per 100,000, Dallas, Texas, was the country's least safe city, rivaling Kolkata as a place to avoid if you value your safety. Yet, many thousands of American businesspeople work in and around Dallas every day, so numbers alone can't make Kolkata all bad.

Cyber Crime

Prompted by concerns about Internet-based crime, India passed the Information Technology (IT) Act in 2000. Several provisions of the IT Act overlap with crimes punishable under the IPC where computers, the Internet, or related aspects were part of the crime, such as legal recognition of electronic records. Examples of cyber crimes under the IT Act include tampering, hacking computer systems, publishing and distributing pornographic and obscene content, unauthorized attempts to access protected computer systems, misrepresentation to obtain a license or digital signature, publishing a false or fraudulent digital signature, and breach of privacy. Examples of cyber crimes under the IPC include offenses by or against public servants, falsifying or destroying electronic evidence, forgery, criminal breach of trust, and counterfeiting. Cyber crime is so new to India that the number of reported cases is, in my opinion, artificially low.

A total of sixty-eight cases were registered under the IT Act in 2004 (compared to sixty in 2003). Of these sixty-eight, 60 percent were related to pornographic/obscene material, 38 percent for hacking, 1 percent for breach of privacy/confidentiality, and 0.2 percent for tampering. One-fourth of the cases occurred in Maharashtra (Mumbai) and the rest from Tamil Nadu (Chennai) and Karnataka (Bangalore). Of the sixty people arrested, 68 percent were between eighteen and thirty years of age.

A total of 279 cyber crime cases were registered under the IPC in 2004 (compared to 411 in 2003). Of these 62 percent were for criminal breach of trust/fraud, 28 percent for forgery, and 10 percent for counterfeiting. Depending on the offense, between 35 percent and 52 percent of the 329 persons arrested were between eighteen and thirty years of age.

It's a little difficult to fathom that so few computer-related crimes took place. Rather, it's much more likely that India has a lot to learn about detecting and prosecuting the illegal activities of cyber criminals.

Part II

Strategic Business Choices and Decisions

Establishing a viable, commercial presence in India can be done in many ways and is constrained, for all intents and purposes, only by a realistic assessment of the business conditions that you'll be operating within. The Central Government provides a fairly clear roadmap toward opportunities for partial or complete investment in most of the country's business sectors. Numerous commercial organizations, government agencies, and global entities are ready to identify, guide, finance, and support promising ventures. Many Western firms have been in India for some time and can offer advice to help you avoid the major pitfalls.

To successfully establish your operation, you should follow a strategic approach. Taking things in small, wait-and-see steps simply will not work. The venture should be planned all the way through to the end; only then will you be prepared to grow and sustain your business. Here are some real examples of issues that should be considered for your plan.

You should start thinking about and identifying alternatives if you rely on rapid inner-city and regional road transportation to meet your customer's demands. Around-the-clock availability of electricity and clean water is uncertain in many parts of India, which will force you to establish your presence in one of the country's newer economic development zones. Even finding English-literate office clerks to handle the routine paperwork or qualified technicians to operate sophisticated manufacturing equipment may be more difficult than you've anticipated.

The remainder of this book takes a hard look at the numerous factors you must consider to make your presence in India a reality, and frames these factors so you can objectively cull their number down to a manageable level. It then guides you in making comprehensive choices with framework decision-making criteria that will help you move in the directions of your goals and enjoy success from your efforts.

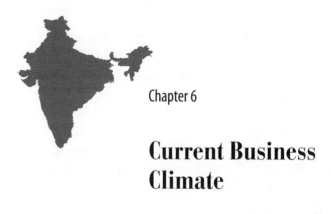

Chapter 6

Current Business Climate

One of the most recent, comprehensive evaluations of current business conditions in India is the World Bank Group's Doing Business 2007 database, which provides reasonably objective measures of business regulations and their enforcement in 175 countries around the world. According to the World Bank, these standardized indicators of the cost of doing business "... measure business regulation and the protection of property rights and their effect on businesses, especially small and medium sized domestic firms . . . by identifying specific regulations that enhance or constrain business investment, productivity and growth." These indicators collectively look at and relatively quantify five macroeconomic criteria considered important in assessing the feasibility of succeeding in a country:

1. The degree of regulation in the economy
2. The quantifiable effect of regulations on business activities
3. The extent of legal protection the business can expect
4. The flexibility of employment regulations
5. The tax burden on businesses

It does this by using templates that specify the size and nature of the business and by using in-country firms to do the following: review specific existing laws and regulations in the economy; conduct interviews with regulators or private-sector professionals; and mine existing data and solicit evaluations and opinions from specialists within the World Bank Group and other third-party group affiliates.

It then develops a score for each of ten indicators for a country that can be compared to other countries in the database to get a feel for the business climate. The indicators are far from perfect, and are developed for wholly owned companies with constraints, but they do help present a picture for each country. Here are the indicators, along with brief summaries of the presumptions used to calculate them:

- **Starting a business:** Assesses official procedures for an entrepreneur to start up and operate a generic Indian business, including procedures, time, cost, and minimum capital requirements. It presumes the business does no activities that entail import/export, accrue special taxes, or cause excessive pollution.
- **Dealing with licenses:** Assesses official procedures, time, and cost for a small-sized construction company to build a standard warehouse in the country's most populated city.
- **Employing workers:** Assesses the feasibility of hiring and firing of workers and the rigidity of working hours at a 200-person manufacturing company located in the country's most populated city.
- **Registering property:** Assesses the full sequence of procedures, including time and cost, for a fifty-person company to purchase the clear title to an existing warehouse for ordinary domestic operations in a suburb of the country's most populated city.
- **Getting credit:** Assesses the legal (collateral and bankruptcy) rights of borrowers and lenders and the sharing of credit information.
- **Protecting investors:** Assesses the strength of minority shareholder protections against director's misuse of

corporate assets for personal gain at a publicly traded company.

- **Paying taxes:** Assesses the tax burden, including bookkeeping and accounting costs, incurred by a medium-sized commercial-products company operating in the country's most populated city. It presumes the business does no activities that entail import/export, accrue special taxes, or cause excessive pollution.
- **Trading across borders:** Assesses the full sequence of official procedures and requirements for exporting and importing a standard (that is, no special requirements, such as refrigeration) cargo of nonmilitary, non-hazardous goods at an Indian-owned, 200-person company operating outside of a tax-haven zone in the country's most populated city.
- **Enforcing contracts:** Assesses the efficiency of the judicial system, in the country's most populated city, in resolving a commercial dispute between two companies about a legal shipment that ended in the plaintiff receiving damaged goods.
- **Closing a business:** Assesses the time, cost, and eventual settlements of bankruptcy proceedings for a founder-owned, 200-employee hotel located in the downtown section of the country's most populated city.

It's very important to emphasize that these indicators look at the effect of regulations on a country's competitiveness, not perceptions or opinions from the business community at-large. The World Bank Group's rationale for taking this approach centers on its mandate to promote growth and expand opportunities for the poor (in other words, to effect sustainable development). So, how does India measure up?

The table on page 106–7 summarizes the scores for a wide range of select countries around the world. It includes countries ranked at the top of the world order, countries popularly called big emerging economies, countries in the less developed world, and countries at the bottom of the world order. (The complete summary, including the entire Doing Business database and its derivation, can be found at the Doing Business Web site, *www.doingbusiness.org.*)

The good news is that India has improved its overall position by four places since the last ranking was published. In this survey, India ranks:

- Ahead of the bottom 25 percent of the 175 countries studied.
- Ahead of 63 percent of these countries in getting credit (ahead of China, Brazil, and Russia).
- Ahead of 81 percent of these countries in protecting investors (again, ahead of China, Brazil, and Russia).
- Ahead of half of these countries for starting a business (well ahead of China and Brazil but behind Russia).
- Below half of the countries for the eight remaining indicators.

Specific global changes in indicator rankings for India since the previous survey are as follows:

- Getting credit improved thirty-one places.
- Starting a business improved fourteen places.
- Employing workers and paying taxes slightly improved by one place.
- Protecting investors, trading across borders, and enforcing contracts were unchanged.
- Dealing with licenses, registering property, and closing a business fell slightly.

In general, this study suggests that India, while still having much room for improvement, is reaping the fruits of earlier efforts to improve the business climate as well as laying the foundation for overall improvements in the years to come. Clearly, taking steps to open the economy to foreign investment should help a great deal. How sincerely and how well India manages this will go a long way toward determining its success.

India's diverse economy encompasses traditional village farming, modern agriculture, handicrafts, a wide range of modern industries, and a multitude of services. Services are the major source of economic growth, accounting for half of India's output with less than 25 percent of its formal labor force; about 65 percent of the entire workforce is in agriculture. (See chapter 2 for information about workforce sectors.)

To ensure political stability, the Central Government is working hard to develop and implement economic-reform programs that include developing basic infrastructure to improve the lives of the rural poor and boost economic performance. Government controls on foreign trade and investment have been reduced in some areas, but high tariffs and limits on foreign direct investment are still in place. Fortunately, the government continues to liberalize investment in nearly all business sectors.

Since 1994, the economy has posted an average growth rate of more than 7 percent, and the government claims to have reduced poverty by about 10 percent, although this is difficult to measure and interpret. The sale of government-owned industries to private investors essentially came to a halt in 2005. This privatization policy continues to cause political debate. The continued social, political, and economic stiffness in the country is affecting population-wide free-market initiatives.

India is seriously trying to significantly expand its manufacturing sector and sees this effort as the lynchpin in its efforts to create jobs for millions of people and to drive exports that will bring in much-needed cash. So far, India has been able to capitalize on its large numbers of well-educated English-speaking people to become a major exporter of IT/BPD services and employer of white-collar workers. Despite India's strong growth, however, the World Bank

Ease of Doing Business in Select Countries

Economy	Ease of Doing Business Rank	Starting a Business	Dealing with Licenses	Employing Workers	Registering Property
Singapore	1	11	8	3	12
United States	3	3	22	1	10
Hong Kong (China)	5	5	64	16	60
United Kingdom	6	9	46	17	19
Ireland	10	6	20	83	80
Japan	11	18	2	36	39
Korea	23	116	28	110	67
Pakistan	74	54	89	126	68
Sri Lanka	89	44	71	98	125
China	93	128	153	78	21
Russia	96	33	163	87	44
Nepal	100	49	127	150	25
Vietnam	104	97	25	104	34
Brazil	121	115	139	99	124
Tajikistan	133	166	85	52	40
India	134	88	155	112	110
Indonesia	135	161	131	140	120
Bhutan	138	79	145	116	41
Haiti	139	167	60	37	135
Cambodia	143	159	159	124	100
Venezuela	164	129	98	165	75
Egypt	165	125	169	144	141
Congo DR	175	172	140	170	141

Source: World Bank Group Doing Business 2007

and other multilateral agencies worry about the combined state and federal budget deficits, which run at approximately 9 percent of GDP. One of the persistent problems is that government borrowing has kept domestic interest rates relatively high. The World Bank feels that economic deregulation would help attract additional foreign capital and reduce inter-

Getting Credit	Protecting Investors	Paying Taxes	Trading Across Borders	Enforcing Contracts	Closing a Business
7	2	8	4	23	2
7	5	62	11	6	16
2	3	5	1	10	14
1	9	12	14	22	10
7	5	2	30	24	7
13	12	98	19	5	1
21	60	48	28	17	11
65	19	140	98	163	46
101	60	157	99	90	59
101	83	168	38	63	75
159	60	98	143	25	81
101	60	88	136	105	95
83	170	120	75	94	116
83	60	151	53	120	135
143	172	154	163	39	50
65	33	158	139	173	133
83	60	133	60	145	136
159	118	68	150	56	151
117	142	87	138	107	146
174	60	161	141	181	51
143	162	167	116	129	144
159	118	144	83	157	120
159	142	147	159	171	145

est rates. However, India's huge and growing population is the fundamental social, economic, and environmental drag.

Regional Economic Performance
Although all of India has benefited from the economic reforms begun in the early 1990s, one only has to follow the trail of money into and out of India to see that the historically

successful and economically powerful states are, once again, the biggest beneficiaries of India's rise to stardom. Most of the recent spectacular economic growth in India is visible in just a few metropolitan areas: Greater Mumbai, in the state of Maharashtra; Bangalore, in the state of Karnataka; Delhi, in the National Capitol Region; and Chennai, in the state of Tamil Nadu. Even within these states and territories, the distribution of wealth is astounding. Great Britain's final abandonment of Calcutta for New Delhi in the early 1900s stunned India's northwest coast, which has not yet seen its fair share of India's economic miracle. Mentioning Kolkata still conjures up images of Mother Teresa caring for the desperately poor in its squalid slums.

Polarizing Progress

Evidence from historical and recent data suggests that the economies of all states and territories in India are growing and that poverty is on the wane. It also suggests that the relative economic rank of states and territories has been quite constant, the distribution of wealth is increasingly polarized, and economic well-being is not related to a state's or territory's population density. Some of the richest states and territories are Delhi, Punjab, Maharashtra, Haryana, Kerala, Gujarat, and Tamil Nadu. An International Monetary Fund worrking paper (WP/06/103) draws some sobering conclusions:

- Income inequality among states is on the rise and has been so for the past thirty years. Nationwide, states with high growth rates grew over twice as fast as those with slow growth rates. The per-capita income of the richest state (Punjab) is presently 4.5 times that of the poorest state (Bihar), up from 3.4 in 1970. Nationwide, the rate at which rich states outgrew poor states was greater than three. The fastest-growing states are those with per-capita incomes around the national average.

- Money trickles down into the lower regions of the economy more efficiently in richer states than in poorer states, for the most part. On average, richer states are about 1.5 times as effective in reducing poverty than poorer states, and the richer they are, the more effective they are.
- Richer states and faster-growing states are better at creating private-sector jobs. Seventy-five percent of Indians employed in the Organized Sector live in high-income and middle-income states. Data from low-income states suggest a net loss of private-sector jobs. Job creation in the public sector has helped soften the blow in low-income states, but it is inadequate to keep pace with the rapidly accelerating private sector.

India is proud of its agrarian heritage. Much of the economy in states and territories located in the northern and interior areas of the country are highly dependent on agriculture, and this is where most of the poorer people live. On the other hand, India's coastal states and territories, which are generally its richest, have long enjoyed the economic benefits of trade, manufacturing, and services concentrated there. It's no surprise that the handful of states with the highest per-capita incomes and with barely 25 percent of the population account for nearly 45 percent of the country's economic activity. States and territories with a viable and diverse middle class are better off, and capital flows easily in their direction. About half of India's total foreign direct investment and over half of its commercial investment is concentrated in its five richest states.

There is speculation that language barriers, poverty, and the lack of extended kinship or family contacts preclude large migrations of workers across long distances and between states. Borders between many states have been drawn on the basis of native language. Indians rely heavily on family and kin for social and economic security. Thus, it appears unlikely that the poor can migrate long distances and across state boundaries in search of work or economic improvement unless they can speak the language of their destination and unless they also have significant, useful personal contacts there—both of which are unlikely. Movement within states, however, is much more common, presumably because these two resources are present in critical amounts. Examples include migration between the adjacent states of Punjab and Delhi and from adjacent or nearby interior states to Maharashtra and Gujarat, where languages are similar and families and kin have had generations to establish viable and sustainable social support networks.

Effects of Concentrated Growth

Could this concentration of growth, which is seemingly restricted to a relatively small area of the country and population, have adverse and long-term consequences for India's economy? Evidence seems to suggest that some of India's booming business sectors are in for a cool-down. There is a real possibility that the existing pool of qualified workers is drying up and those already employed will demand higher wages as they become more aware of their value. Other emerging countries are aggressively courting U.S. and European multinationals, hoping to get a sizeable piece of the pie.

Will India's inability in finding, producing, and mobilizing qualified workers from the poorer rural states to jobs in Delhi, Maharashtra, Bangalore, and Chennai jeopardize its economic future? Can India's marginalized poor wait forever? They might, but their militant champions in the various factions of the Communist Party of India will not.

Better known as Naxalites, with organized groups in over 100 districts in twelve of India's twenty-eight states, these guerilla-style insurgents pose a real concern to the Central Government. Already operating in Nepal, Naxalites were responsible for igniting that country's eleven-year-long civil war, which resulted in the deaths of nearly 13,000 Nepalese and the abductions of over 100,000 more. The war ended in November 2006 with the overthrow of the monarchy and the signing of a peace agreement between the Maoist rebel forces and the new military government.

Themselves a collection of disjointed groups with a classless society as their goal, Naxalites in India claim to be waging a bloody war against the oppression and exploitation practiced by prominent and wealthy landlords on behalf of serf-like landless laborers, lower-caste workers, and tribal people. Their critics say the Naxalites are nothing more than organized criminals, extorting money and protection from upper-caste landowners, and opportunistic terrorists, using class war as their excuse to oppress defenseless people. Although a very small minority in the country, the Naxalites' persistence feeds the underlying tension among the hundreds of millions of India's poor and young people who are still waiting for the economic miracle to come knocking on their doors.

The U.S. Central Intelligence Agency points toward several more groups as potentially destabilizing to civil authority. These include numerous religious or militant/chauvinistic organizations, including Vishwa Hindu Parishad, Bajrang Dal, and Rashtriya Swayamsevak Sangh; and various separatist groups seeking greater communal and/or regional autonomy, including the All Parties Hurriyat Conference in the Kashmir Valley and the National Socialist Council of Nagaland in the Northeast.

Workforce, Skills, and Education

One of the great uncertainties in India is the depth and flexibility of its workforce. The majority of India's population is engaged in agrarian activities, be it as seasonal employees of a larger concern or as part of a family or village operation. In states with hot economies and burgeoning rosters of recent college and technical school graduates, such as Maharashtra, agricultural workers often migrate from farming areas into expanding metropolitan areas in search of unskilled-labor jobs. When the planting season rolls around, they simply migrate back.

A look at the demand for consumer goods shows that a true middle class is establishing itself in and around India's hottest metropolitan areas. These people bring with them all the skills and education familiar to many Americans. Recent estimates put the size of this emerging middle class and the people dependent on it at up to 325 million, nearly 30 percent of the country's entire population.

One might wonder if, in a country of over a billion people, employers could ever run out of workers. Evidence suggests it could. The continued growth in technology-based services, the addition of new skills and services, and industry's hopes for a globally competitive manufacturing sector are beginning to uncover some of the limitations in India's skilled and educated population. The fact that half of the population is younger than twenty-five says a lot about available talent, too. Already, tech firms are scrambling to fill the domestic demand for qualified knowledge workers. Which business sector will be the next to feel the pinch, one that's already well established or something new and exciting that's still over the horizon?

Meeting the Demand for Skilled Workers

There are several factors at play here and they must all be synchronized to ensure that India's workers, present and future, can meet the demands of its growing economy and support its role in the global marketplace. For much of the country's history, education in India was a privilege. Constrained by age-old prejudices and discriminations, the majority of India's children only had access to educational opportunities commensurate with their anticipated future role in society. Thus, on one end of the spectrum, few if any farmers received more than a rudimentary schooling in arithmetic and grammar, while on the other end most Brahmins lived a life bathed in the highest education the country could offer.

Many upper-caste members earned advanced degrees while studying overseas in Europe, the United Kingdom, and the United States. For most of the twentieth century, and especially since Independence, there has been a steady brain drain as educated, intelligent Indians looked to foreign lands for the opportunities and rewards they could not find at home. Few of these emigrants have ever moved back and neither state governments nor the Central Government have made repatriation a priority, largely due to India's pressing overpopulation problem.

Beginning in the 1980s, the intrinsic value of the Indian people as a national resource in the country's growth and its future success became increasingly important to the Central Government. In 1985, the Ministry of Human Resource Development was created from a collection of mostly inefficient agencies and given the mission of integrating and standardizing state and central educational agencies and resources. Its goal is to provide education and training for all Indians from childhood through the rest of life.

Education and Unemployment

A casual look at the fruits of India's educational system is revealing. Of persons in the worker pool between the ages of fifteen and fifty-nine, the following average statistics hold true:

- 8.3 percent do not have a primary education (completed school through the age of eleven).
- 14.4 percent have no more than a primary education.
- 12 percent have at least some secondary education.
- 7.8 percent have completed a secondary education.

- 0.6 percent have completed some form of technical certification administered by the Ministry of Human Resource Development.
- Less than 0.1 percent have completed some form of non-technical certification.

Also, on average, 6.8 percent of persons who completed secondary school (at least twenty years of age) have gone on to complete university and graduate schools.

The data also shows that the future is brighter, provided that the ministry can keep students in the educational pipeline. The percentage of students completing successively higher degrees of education is increasingly greater for younger students, clearly indicating that more and more of India's people are getting access to education. At the same time, huge numbers of India's people are children of primary-school age, which bodes well for the distant future.

However, this success in the educational system is a double-edged sword. The population-growth rate of working aged persons between fifteen and sixty years of age is rising and won't level off for several years, according to Central Government projections. This rate exceeds the overall population growth rate, putting real pressure on the economy to generate jobs.

So far, India's economic boom has apparently been able to absorb this increasing number of workers. However, two other factors will play a role, although to what extent is still uncertain. As Central Government efforts to jump-start the educational system continue to take hold, more and more children will find their way from the farm and factory to the classroom. This is already clear. At the same time, more and more women, who are woefully underrepresented in the workforce (by Western standards), will be looking for jobs in both urban and rural areas that have traditionally been off limits to them. Their presence in the newer jobs is already significant, especially among educated women in the fastest-growing states.

On average, the Central Government estimates that around 2 million persons will be added to the unemployment rolls each year for the immediate future. With unemployment currently around 9 percent, the key question is, "How many more unemployed people can the economy support?" Furthermore, underemployment in the workforce (such as in rural farming areas where work is seasonal) is estimated at around 9 percent, with an estimated 13 percent for school-aged young people. In total, India is facing estimated unemployment and underemployment rates in the range of 18 percent of the workforce and over 20 percent of school-aged young people.

Agriculture Workforce

The Central Government is especially sensitive to conditions in states where the local and regional economies are heavily dependent on agriculture. Pressure has greatly increased to use arable land more efficiently. As modern agribusiness techniques and equipment come into use in greater and greater numbers, so will the demand for a technically skilled workforce to implement and operate them. However, India's educational shortcomings are at their greatest in these very locations, and this could constrain the pace of modernization. Where this is the case, how will people be told about a reality in which jobs as manual laborers are the only options they have? More importantly, will they accept this explanation? Clearly, worker unrest and regional political stability are on the government's mind.

Infrastructure

India's national infrastructure is continuously undergoing tremendous change. Money is pouring into capital projects from the government as well as private sources. Investment portfolios have been accumulating more and more infrastructure instruments as firms in the sector book orders at a record pace. Yet India's antiquated infrastructure still hangs like a millstone around its neck. Commuters can sit for hours in traffic getting to and from the office. In Bangalore, Western firms have threatened to or have even pulled out of projects and joint ventures due to their perception that it's literally impossible to get around with any kind of efficiency. India is working hard to overcome this liability, but hundreds of years of malaise cannot be jump-started overnight.

Elephants and camels are still used for transportation, although not in newer urban areas. Roads, railroads, shipping ports, and airports continue to expand. India has the world's second-largest road network, and its historically overcrowded rail network is likely the most used in the world. Increasing incomes and looser government policies have contributed to tremendous growth in the numbers of automobiles, two- and three-wheeled vehicles, private and public buses, and urban rail networks. However, this growth has accelerated problems with pollution, increased traffic density, allowed for unlicensed and uninsured transporters, and resulted in many more traffic accidents and fatalities.

Highways

One of India's greatest civil engineering and construction projects has been the Golden Quadrilateral. Part of the ongoing National Highways Development Project to build four- and six-lane expressways connecting important areas of the country, the 3,500-mile long Golden Quadrilateral is India's national ring road. It connects major metropolitan areas in Delhi, Bangalore, Mumbai, Chennai, and Kolkata and serves as the jumping-off point to other major highways to the north, northeast, east, south, and central areas of the country. Besides the Central Government, the private sector is getting involved in developing for-profit road systems. Also, a variety of projects to improve road infrastructure are in progress with support from the World Bank, which is one of the main money providers to India, as well as the Asian Development Bank.

Exclusive of the Golden Quadrilateral, the *CIA World Factbook* (2006) reports there are about 2.31 million miles of roads in India. Of this, 1.45 million miles are paved with some form of hard, load-bearing surface and 864,000 are unpaved. Some sources indicate that as much as 60 percent of India's passenger and freight traffic uses less than 2 percent of the country's roads, all of it in bad condition. Over 100 national highways carry about 40 percent of the country's road traffic on their 39,340 miles. Around 85 percent of all passenger traffic and 70 percent of all freight traffic travels by road. Urban transit is dominated by motor vehicles, motorcycles, and bicycles, with pack animals still used in many areas, including cities.

Railroads

India is either famous or infamous for its railroads, depending on where or when you've last ridden on them. Since the early 1990s, the government has significantly modernized parts of the railway system, but dwindling financial support and protectionist policies of equipment manufacturers regularly takes a toll.

The first stretch of railroad in India was laid down in 1853 between Mumbai and Thane—all of twenty-one miles apart. Since then the rail lines have grown to cover 37,938 route miles. Counting multiple tracks in common rights-of-way results in a total track length of 65,200 miles. Of the total route-miles, 27,430 miles of track (72 percent) is 1.676-meter gauge, 8,643 miles (32 percent) is 1.000-meter gauge, and 1,836 miles (5 percent) is 0.762- and 0.610-meter gauge. About 9,900 miles of track is electrified, mostly 1.676-meter gauge. It is estimated that there are nearly 116,000 bridges in the system.

All zonal railroad systems are owned by the government and operated by Indian Railways. The fourth most heavily used rail system in the world, Indian Railways operates nearly 15,000 trains a day. It carries over 1 million metric tons of freight and 14 million passengers on 8,700 trains between 6,856 stations and countless depots. In recent years annual loads have exceeded 500 million freight-tons and more than 5 billion passengers. In 2002 the Central Government kicked off the National Rail Vikas Yojana plan. This massive investment, intended to open up the country and unclog the existing system, will see the following:

- Construction of new lines and upgrades of existing lines in and between the major metropolitan areas of Delhi, Mumbai, Chennai, and Kolkata.
- Construction of four river bridges at Patna and Munger on the Ganges, at Bogibeel on the Brahmaputra, and at Nirmali on the Kosi.
- Development of multi-modal corridors between major ports and rural areas.

India also has a few high-speed routes and several urban passenger rail systems. Kolkata has a full metro system, and New Delhi's metro system is operational and expanding. Chennai has a rapid-transit system, and there are suburban rail networks in Bangalore, Mumbai, and New Delhi. Over the coming years, riders will see increasing availability of metro and light-rail in Bangalore, Mumbai, Coimbatore, Hyderabad, Jaipur, Lucknow, and Pune.

Ports and Terminals

India has up to eleven major seaports, depending on the criteria. These are overseen by boards appointed by India's Ministry of State for Surface Transport, but they are managed by semi-independent port trusts, including the navy, port labor and port industry, and ship owners and shipping companies. These ports are Kandla, Mumbai, Nhava Sheva (Jawaharlal Nehru Port Trust), Marmagao/Panaji, New Mangalore, and Kochi (Cochin) on the west coast; on the east coast are Kolkata (Calcutta-Haldia), Paradip, Vishakhapatnam, Chennai, and Tuticorin. A twelfth, Ennore Port, was originally conceived as a coal-handling facility to supply electricity generation throughout Tamil Nadu—its motto is "Energy Port of the New Millennium"—and Ennore India's first port being run as a corporate venture. Total port traffic nationwide is estimated at nearly 500 million tons, with the major ports accounting for around three-quarters of the traffic.

There also are hundreds of minor and intermediate ports along the coastline and on offshore islands that are administered by local, state, or union territory maritime authorities. There are seven shipyards under the control of the Central Government, two shipyards controlled by state governments, and nineteen shipyards that are privately owned. Most of the over 100 shipping companies operating in India are owned by state and local governments. Five are privately owned and one, the Shipping Corporation of India, Ltd., is a Government of India Enterprise. There are over 300 multimodal transport operators in India, which is one of the few countries that has a separate law for multimodal transportation. Under the Multimodal Transportation of Goods Act of 1993, the Directorate-General of Shipping is the agency for registering multimodal transport operators in India. In 2003, Indian-flagged vessels reportedly carried about 15 percent of overseas cargo into and out of Indian ports.

Inland and Coastal Waterways

According to official Indian sources, the country has approximately 8,700 miles of inland waterways, but the transportation potential is vastly underused. Of the 3,120 miles on major rivers, more than 2,160 miles are navigable by large vessels, although only about 1,200 miles are routinely used. River traffic also is important on the Ganges, Brahmaputra, Narmada, and Godovari rivers, as well as 290 miles of commercially navigable canals.

The National Waterways Project envisions a network of national waterways linking major parts of the country in the same manner that the Golden Quadrilateral is projected to form the basis of a national highway system. By constructing sophisticated canals and dredging parts of existing waterways, India hopes to create three east-west waterway zones: the Himalayan, Central, and Southern. Intended to benefit the states, various master plans have been conceived and rejected due to concerns about sharing water rights, flood control, downstream impacts from agriculture and irrigation, navigation, hydroelectric power, and environmental and resource conservation. So far, the project includes three inland waterways: 972 miles of the Allahabad-Haldia portion of the Ganga-Bhagirathi-Hooghly rivers; 535 miles of the Sadiya-Dhubri section of the Brahmaputra River; and 123 miles created from a combination of western canals.

Airports and Aviation

Fifty domestic and international airlines operate flights to and within India, with services ranging from gold plated to those that appeal only to the most adventuresome thrill-seekers. The government operates two airlines, Air India and Indian Airlines, and one helicopter service, Pawan Hans. Private airlines account for about half of domestic air traffic and, as of 2003, the government had divested more than 50 percent of its equity in both government-owned airlines. There are several privately owned airlines, including the fast-rising Jet Airlines and Kingfisher Airlines. Air travel is relatively new in India, with its 341 registered airports. Of these, 71 percent are paved. How do India's airport services compare to some other countries?

Paved Airports and Heliports by Country

	United States	India	China	Brazil
Total heliports	149	28	32	417
Total airports	14,858	341	486	4,276
Paved	5,119	243	403	714
>10,000 ft.	189	17	56	8
8,000 to 10,000 ft.	221	51	127	24
5,000 to 7,999 ft.	1,426	73	138	164
3,000 to 4,999 ft.	2,337	81	22	464
< 3,000 ft.	946	21	60	54

Source: CIA World Factbook (2006)

The Airports Authority of India administers 126 airports: eleven international, eighty-nine domestic, and twenty-six defense-related with civilian components. In 2003 these airports collectively handled approximately 500,000 flights, 40 million passengers, and 900,000 tons of cargo. Major international airports are located in Kolkata, Chennai, Mumbai, New Delhi, and Thiruvananthapuram. There also is international service from Bangalore, Guwahati, Hyderabad, and Mamargao, and there are major regional airports at Ahmadabad, Allahabad, Chandigarh, Kochi (Cochin), Nagpur, Pune, Srinagar, and Thiruvananthapuram.

Fuel Pipelines

India has an estimated 3,110 miles of gas pipelines, 1,200 miles for liquid petroleum gas, 3,900 miles for oil, and 3,700 miles for refined products. Iran and Pakistan have been discussing construction of a gas pipeline to bring natural gas from Iran to India on and off for several years, although security concerns are still high.

Telecommunications

In telecommunications, India is seeing the greatest change in any of its business sectors. Deregulation and liberalization of telecommunications laws and policies have sprouted hundreds of private service providers as well as greater public use of a variety of existing services. For example, recent estimates put the number of Internet users at around 50 million and the number of Internet hosts at near 2,000,000.

Telephone

Local and long-distance telephone service is generally available throughout the country, although services are primarily concentrated in urbanized areas. Nationwide, there is a waiting list of over 1.7 million for fixed line service. There is steady improvement taking place in rural areas with the recent admission of private investors and private-public joint ventures in the sector. Traditional telephone coverage remains low, by Western standards, at about seven for each 100 persons nationwide but only one per 100 persons in rural areas, where cellular services are making significant inroads.

By far the fastest growth is in cellular services. First introduced in 1994, the industry was organized nationwide into four metropolitan city and nineteen telecom circles, each with about three private service providers and one state-owned service provider. Much of this growth has been driven by increased competition and dramatic reductions in price. In 2004, there were an estimated 40.9 million telephones and 26.2 million cellular phones. In 2003, there were an estimated 7.5 million personal computers in use—which could be as high as 20 million if this sector grows at a rate comparable to that of Internet users. It's also very possible that Voice over Internet Protocol (VoIP) telephone services may grow faster than fixed telephone services because India has added significant trunk capacity in the form of fiber-optic cable.

Satellite and Radio

India has one of the world's largest domestic satellite systems and is the largest in the Asia-Pacific region. The Indian National Satellite system (INSAT) has nine satellites carrying about 150 transponders, which supports telecommunications, broadcasting, weather and emergency-response needs.

The government-owned radio (All India Radio) and television (Doordarshan) networks have extensive national and local coverage, but domestic and international private television networks are proliferating through the extensive use of cable and satellite. According to government figures, there were 79.4 million households with television in 2001. From 1991 to 2002, the number of radios roughly doubled to an estimated 111 million, and radio remains the main source of news for most Indians.

Financial Stability

Indian fiscal and monetary thinking has come a long way since the persistent budget deficits of the 1980s and the foreign exchange crisis in 1991, when the country came to the brink of bankruptcy. Staring into the abyss, the Central Government took several major steps that turned things around. It worked hard to bring domestic spending into line with tax and other revenues, loosened restrictions and artificial valuations of the rupee, and began the crucial undertaking of opening the country's economy for foreign investment while placating as much of traditional business as possible. The most successful product of these policies has been India's high-tech industry, which has made millionaires out of more than a few people and laid the foundation for a small but new middle class whose lifestyles are certain to spread their wealth to other socioeconomic strata.

Salary Pressure

In late 2006, the Central Government published figures showing India's average salary increase, at 13.8 percent, was the highest in the Asia-Pacific region, far surpassing Philippines (in second place) at 8.3 percent and China (in third place) at 8 percent. Future increases of average overall salaries are anticipated in the 12.3 to 15 percent range, with senior and top level managers looking forward to 20 percent increases. While high, these are far more rational than in past years and still behind the pace of Singapore, Thailand, and Malaysia.

The employee turnover rate at Indian tech services firms is staggering. Demand for qualified workers is outstripping supply, and employees are jumping jobs for a 10 (or more) percent raise every three or four months. Other countries in the Asia-Pacific region are scrambling to fill the gaps. (Even Native American Indians, such as the Umatilla Tribe in eastern Washington State, have signed service agreements with U.S. firms to provide similar services.) Many U.S. and European companies are closely watching these developments. However, it's unlikely that U.S. capital will be fleeing India anytime soon.

Macroeconomic Factors

The Asian Development Bank generally feels India's future is bright, although some bumps may be encountered, and expects the economy to grow at around 8 percent for the next several years. Industrial growth is expected to be similar to this rate, while the services sector is expected to grow even faster. On the downside, agriculture will expand more slowly, at only around 2 percent, even though increased energy costs are a smaller component of this sector. Agriculture is far more sensitive to weather than most other sectors, so any significant downward departures from normal rainfall and monsoon activity would affect every level of the national economy. The bank also expects that there will be some wholesale price inflation and that India's trade deficit will continue.

At times public debt has accounted for 90 percent of the GDP. Despite increasingly positive economic results, India remains a poor country. India's presence in global trade, although on the rise, is still that of a minor player at less than 1 percent of the world's exports. India's main trading partners are the United States, the United Arab Emirates, and China. The International Monetary Fund forecasts continued growth, and most of the other economic indicators are favorable.

The economy currently stands among the world's fourth-largest growing economy, as calculated by purchasing power parity, and holds the distinction of being a key contributor to Asia's net balance-of-payment surplus. Capital inflows have remained large during FY 2006–2007. Inflows of foreign equity capital investments into India during the first quarter were up nearly 50 percent over the same period in the preceding year, and were up 102 percent early in the second quarter over the same period in the preceding year. And, according to a survey of global investor confidence by A.T. Kearney, India is the second-most attractive country in the world for foreign investors.

Banking and Finance

The banking sector also has been reinventing itself in support of this growth and is continuing to lay the foundation for the future. Embracing its responsibility to all the people of India as monitor of the country's financial stability, the Reserve Bank of India regularly announces new reforms, initiatives, and policies that it believes will make India much more attractive to foreign investors. The bank has focused its efforts on controlling inflation and stabilizing financial institutions, financial markets, and the financial infrastructure.

While tech services have led the country's emergence onto the world's stage, India's economic and social future is tied to its own domestic economy. As noted above, the incredible pay increases enjoyed by a small part of the population rarely trickle down very far. How well or how poorly

India plays this hand could mean the difference between life and death for millions of its citizens. One new component of the banking sector that goes directly to the country's social bottom line is microfinance.

First introduced in Bangladesh in 1976, the concept of microfinance works by loaning small amounts to the very poor as seed capital for entrepreneurial ventures, such as the purchase by a rural villager of a cell phone that's then offered for fee-based use to fellow villagers. Microfinance is taking off in India, and current estimates are on track for it to match the pace of loans seen across the border, where nearly 7 million Bangladeshis, of whom 97 percent are women, have already done so. The best news is that even though the amounts are tiny, the occurrence of bad loans is said to be far less than that experienced by traditional banks.

Agriculture

Agriculture provides about 28 percent of the GDP, with almost two-thirds of the active population involved in the sector, and India has the largest supplies of livestock in the world. India is the second-largest food producer in the world, with an annual production exceeding 210 million metric tons. It ranks first in the world in the production of milk, tea, sugarcane, and spices. It is the second-largest producer of fruits, vegetables, rice, wheat, tobacco, and nuts (such as peanuts and cashews) and is among the top five producers of coffee, spices, cereals, and oil seeds. India produces nearly half of the world's mangos, one-fourth of the world's bananas and cashew nuts, and a third of the world's cauliflower and green peas.

Mining and Minerals

Ore and raw materials resources also are important. Coal is the country's principal source of energy (India is the world's fourth-largest producer of coal), although increased domestic demand for chemicals and fuels has driven up imports of petroleum and gas.

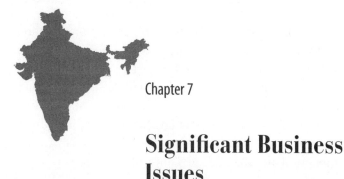

Chapter 7

Significant Business Issues

India presents many unique challenges to the Western business person. Here in the United States, we're accustomed to starting, growing, and managing businesses under a mantle of well understood and controlled conditions. Worker absenteeism due to illness is very low. Water from the tap in the office kitchen is clean and freely flows 24 hours a day, 7 days a week; and so does abundant electricity. America has the means to respond to and survive virtually any natural disaster. Indians do not enjoy the same standard of living that we do. Decades of uncontrolled municipal practices and unchecked population growth have exposed India's soft underbelly, leaving its people less protected from day-to-day occurrences that you or I wouldn't even think about it.

These issues are far from insurmountable, but having a comfortable awareness of them is invaluable.

Public Health and Health Care

National statistics show that the health and well-being of India's people is improving. Yet, like many other modern things about the country, significant investments in India's public health and health-care systems tend to follow the money trail in and around those major metropolitan areas enjoying the biggest economic growth. In booming cities like Chennai, Hyderabad, Mumbai, and New Delhi, India's blue-chip corporations have built sophisticated private hospitals to care for the emerging elite and anyone else who can afford to pay the bill, including Americans, Europeans, and Asians. Getting patched up in an Indian hospital is amazingly cheap compared to what it costs in the West.

Since 1991, health-care financial and technical resources, and the number of health-care professionals, have significantly increased in size and availability. Yet insiders know this is just the tip of the iceberg. Today, still, much of rural and poor India relies on indigenous and traditional medical practices, such as herbal and Ayurvedic (spiritual) medicines. Once frowned upon as the realm of jungle witchdoctors, today's alternative-medicine sector enjoys formal recognition by the Central Government, is gaining in popularity, and graduates thousands of new practitioners from Unani and Ayurvedic colleges each year.

India on the World Health Stage

Where, then, does India rank on the world's public health scale? According to data collected by the World Health Organization from 2001 to 2006, India has a critical shortage of health-care workers.

Doctors, Nurses, and Other Select Health Professionals (Per Capita)

	United States	India	China
Physicians	2.56 (730,801)	0.6 (645,825)	1.06 (1,364,000)
Nurses	9.37 (2,669,603)	0.8 (865,135)	1.05 (1,358,000)
Dentists	1.63 (463,663)	0.06 (592,577)	0.11 (136,520)
Pharmacists	0.88 (249,642)	0.56 (592,577)	0.28 (359,000)
Other Health Workers	14.66 (4,177,609)	0.76 (818,301)	0.82 (1,061,000)
Health Management and Support Workers	24.76 (7,056,080)	"no data"	0.83 (1,077,000)

Note: Figures in parentheses are numbers of individuals

Source: World Health Organization's Core Health Indicators—2006

How do health-care costs in India compare with America and some other emerging countries? Data suggests expenditures are far lower, although the reasons for this are subtle and buried within the inefficiencies of India's socioeconomic system.

Health Care Expenditures

	United States	India	China	Brazil
Per capita ($)	6,096	91	277	1,520
Total (percent of GDP)	15.4	5.0	4.7	8.8
Government contribution (percentage)	44.7	17.3	38.0	54.1
Percentage of all government expenditures	18.9	2.9	18.1	14.2
Private contribution (percentage)	55.3	82.7	62.0	45.9
Out of pocket (percentage of private contribution)	23.8	93.8	86.5	64.2

Source: World Health Organization's Core Health Indicators—2007

In India, 78 percent of the cost of health care comes directly out of the individual's pocket, putting it far down the list of countries providing health care for its citizens. In the United States, the health-care burden is much more equally shared between the government and the private sector. The Center on Enquiry into Health and Allied Themes (*www.cehat.org*) calls the public health-care system in India abysmal and in a state of collapse since the economic crisis of the 1990s, when the government started turning away from pre-Independence socialist ideals of comprehensive and universal coverage to doing little more than struggling to provide funds for family planning, immunization, disease surveillance, medical education, and research. The private sector's pay-as-you-go business model cannot fill the gap, especially for the huge numbers of rural and urban poor whose populations are ravaged by largely preventable infections. Also, inadequate inoculations against diseases like hepatitis, polio, and tuberculosis leave large segments of the population at substantial risk.

The Social Price of Health Care in India

The reduction in public health spending and the growing inequalities in health care are taking a toll on the marginalized and socially disadvantaged population. Does moving from a rural state to a metropolitan area make a difference? The data says no. The frequency of all illnesses, infant mortality, malnutrition, access to hospitals, and pre-natal care are significantly higher in economically depressed urban areas of the country.

Key Life-Expectancy Indicators (Per 1000 population)

	World Average[1]	India	U.S.	World Highs	World Lows
Birth Rate[2]	20	22[93]	14[156]	45 (Africa)	8 (Europe/Hong Kong)
Death Rate[2]	8.7	8.18[112]	8.26[107]	29 (Africa)	2.5 (Middle East)
Life Expectancy	64.8	64.7[164]	77.9[48]	80+ years (Asia/Australia/Europe)	40 years (Africa)
Frequency of HIV/AIDS (adults)	–	0.9[59]	0.6[71]	20+ (Southern Africa)	0 (Several)

Notes: (1) Out of 227 countries; (2) India's birth and death rates are biased due to the extraordinarily low average age of its population.
Numbers in brackets are the country's world rank out of 222 countries.
Source: CIA World Factbook—2006

According to official estimates, 5.15 million Indians are infected with HIV/AIDS, and each year well over 300,000 die. In both of these categories, India has the dubious distinction of ranking second in the world behind only South Africa.

Environmental Degradation

By Western standards, India's overall environmental management and protection record has been below par. The ongoing population explosion, urbanization, and industrialization have placed enormous stress on the country's natural resources. In rural India, soil erosion, deforestation, land degradation, and water pollution are holding back economic development, while urbanization and industrialization are causing serious air pollution and are overwhelming municipal systems' ability to deliver water and remove wastes.

India, herself, points to several key drivers that the nation must get under control to avoid significant impacts on its long-term success: population growth; unwise consumption and technology practices; poverty; and development practices. These factors have perpetuated environmental degradation through institutional failures, market failures, and governance constraints. Inadequacies in laws, regulations, and institutions have accelerated environmental degradation, as have delays and increased costs in development projects.

Environmental Awakening

India traces its national environmental awareness to the early 1970s. Prior to then, environmental policy was largely decided in the courts using a few antiquated laws and was the result of claims made against nuisances or negligence. The Wild Life Protection Act in 1972 and the Water (Prevention and Control of Pollution) Act of 1974 were the first statutes that could be used to develop an environmental protection policy from. These were followed by the Water Cess Act in 1977, the Forest (Conservation) Act in 1980, and the Air (Prevention and Control of Pollution) Act in 1981. In 1984, the death of tens of thousands of Indians in Bhopal from the release of a highly toxic chemical galvanized world opinion as to the undeniable interrelationship between humans and the environment. The Central Government passed the Environment (Protection) Act in 1986, which created India's Ministry of Forests and Environment. The ministry works closely with a host of other ministries, such as urban development, water resources, and women and child development, to name only a few, to design and implement environmental policy and goals. In 1997, the National Environment Appellate Authority Act established the National Environment Appellate Authority, which hears appeals against orders granting environmental clearance in designated areas where industrial activity is restricted under the Environment Act. The authority has been a lightening rod for friction between pro-development and pro-environment groups since its inception, and many cases have ultimately made their way to India's Supreme Court. For example, the Biodiversity Act was passed in 2002.

Sustainable Development

In 2006, India proclaimed its first national environmental policy, which builds on earlier sector and issue specific policies. Intended as a framework and living document to guide existing and future development, the policy unabashedly wraps its arms around the universal principals of sustainable development as crafted and defined by the United Nations. Its key principals include the following:

- All of India's people, present and future, are entitled to healthy and productive lives.
- All polluters will be held accountable for environmental damage.
- A polluter's liability will be fault-based and strict.

The strategies and actions to accomplish this are an interesting blend of Western pragmatism and Eastern philosophy: regulatory reform; enhancement and conservation of environmental resources; development and adherence to environmental standards; introduction and implementation of clean and innovative technologies; promotion of environmental awareness, education, and information; identification, promotion, and supporting involvement of partners and stakeholders; growth of the capacity to support environmental protection; pursuit of new ways through focused research and development; and technology import and export through international cooperation on the environment.

India's Huge Environmental Burden

At present, India supports more than 16 percent of the world's people on 2.5 percent of the world's land. Massive overcrowding in the cities has overshadowed the burden that its growing population places on arable land—the population density on arable land is about twice that of the national average. Technological advances have greatly increased India's agricultural efficiency, yet the United Nations Environmental Program (UNEP) points out that 90 percent of the increased demand for food comes directly from the increased population and only 10 percent from higher living standards. Equally ominous, the availability of non-recycled fresh water is less than half of what it was fifty years ago. Meanwhile, India's population has tripled in the last fifty years and is still increasing, yet half the country's citizens are no older than twenty-five. Clearly, the environmental pressures on India are enormous and are not going away.

Air Pollution

Air pollution is arguably India's most severe environmental concern as it has the biggest impact on the public health and contributes to global warming. Of all countries in the world, India has the dubious distinction of annually claiming the most premature deaths attributable to outdoor and indoor air pollution. Industrialization and urbanization have caused a massive deterioration of India's air quality, largely as a result of emissions from motor vehicles and industrial facilities. According to the U.S. Department of Energy, the skies above India's four major cities of Mumbai, Chennai, Kolkata, and Delhi are among the world's most polluted.

Although India's environmental regulations are comprehensive, the pandemic lack of municipal involvement and local regulatory enforcement has been the major roadblock to improving conditions. In major metropolitan areas, federal regulations and even rulings handed down by the Indian

Supreme Court have been ignored or shelved for a variety of less-than-legitimate reasons.

As might be predicted, social unrest has been one result of a population pushed to the limits of its patience. Citizens of New Delhi grew so frustrated with the lack of progress that they took matters into their own hands. When a court-imposed deadline for replacing diesel- and gasoline-powered vehicles with buses powered by natural gas was missed and tens of thousands of vehicles were banned from the roads, they protested and rioted to such an extent that the commutation systems were thrown into complete chaos.

Water Shortages and Pollution

According to the United States Agency for International Development (USAID), Indians account for 13 percent of the world's population suffering from potable water shortages and 43 percent of the world's population suffering from sanitation shortages. Water shortages are exacerbated by the inefficiencies of the water delivery systems. Part of the blame for this rests squarely on the shoulders of the municipal governments, none of which has demonstrated the ability to develop or manage a comprehensive program to reduce loss of water and revenues in its delivery systems. USAID also estimates that some utilities literally flush up to half of their potential revenues through leaking pipes, illegal connections, and unpaid bills.

The World Health Organization has presented cost-benefit analyses that underscore the importance that improved environmental conditions might have on the future economic strength of India. On the basis of a dollar invested, the organization offers these examples of economic benefits that could be realized:

- Providing access to piped connections for regulated water and sewer for all households yields a benefit of at least $2.90.

- Halving the proportion of people without access to both improved water supply and improved sanitation yields a benefit of $3.16.
- Providing access to improved water and improved sanitation services for all households yields a benefit of at least $7.88.
- Providing access to an improved water and sanitation service, plus household water treatment at point-of-use for all households, yields a benefit of at least $9.41.

Dealing with industrial water pollution problems will be far more difficult due to the huge number of sources.

Energy Security

Since 1980, India's energy consumption has more than tripled, largely due to the increases in population and rapid urbanization. Yet, with over a billion people, India's per-capita consumption of energy is quite low. According to the U.S. Department of Energy, higher energy consumption in the industrial, transportation, and residential sectors is driving India's energy usage upward at a rate faster than even China's, whose energy consumption increased nearly 2.5 times during the same period. Projections of annual average increases in energy use for the period from 2003 to 2030 have India at 3.8 percent, just behind China at 5 percent and other developing Asian countries at 4.5 percent. Among other emerging markets, Brazil is expected to grow at 2.9 percent, Mexico at 2.8 percent, South Korea at 2.5 percent, and Russia at 2.4 percent. (The United States lags behind at 1.5 percent.)

Globally, India ranks sixth with 2.3 percent of energy production; the United States is first, with 21 percent. India's current use of energy is relatively low compared to more industrialized countries at: 89 percent that of Germany, 58 percent that of Japan, 32 percent that of China, and 13 percent that of the United States.

Sources of Energy

According to India's International Energy Agency, India generates 80 percent of all of its energy from domestic sources and estimates are that half of that comes from traditional fuels, such as wood, biomass, cattle dung, human excrement, agricultural wastes, and processing of byproducts. Much of India's rural population, which accounts for around 70 percent of the entire population, relies almost exclusively on these traditional fuels. India generates its primary and commercial energy largely from coal (51 percent) and the rest from petroleum (34 percent), natural gas (7 percent), hydroelectric (6 percent), and nuclear (2 percent).

Natural gas usage has been growing in importance, as seen by India's recent negotiations with Iran and Pakistan to build a natural-gas pipeline through both countries, while hydroelectric has been in decline, owing to increased sensitivity to the enormous and widespread impacts from construction and operation of large dams. Interestingly, India's first major irrigation and hydroelectric dam project, the enormous Bhakra Nangal Dam in Punjab, was the biggest factor leading to the state of Punjab becoming the wealthiest in India.

India's reserves of natural gas and oil are low by global standards. However, India is just behind China and the United States with the world's third-largest reserves of coal. The majority use of coal burning is for generating electricity, at a rate about twice that of the world's average. To support economic growth projections, the Central Government foresees huge increases in electricity generated from coal. However, it's not certain that India's coal reserves can meet this demand without major investments in technology: Her coal is relatively low in fuel value and has a high inert content.

India currently imports about 70 percent of its oil, and the International Energy Agency projects that demand will increase to over 90 percent by 2020. Overall, India gets about 65 percent of its energy inputs from the Persian Gulf. As noted above, India is negotiating with Iran for gas supplies and also is reaching out to Tajikistan, Kazakhstan, and Azerbaijan in hopes of negotiating strategic relationships for fuel. India recently entered into a cooperative agreement with China to partner in oil exploration and production in Africa.

National Security

India's approach to national security has evolved over the past fifteen years. National defense by a competent and well-supplied military is still first and foremost in the country's plans. However, portraying itself as one of the future leaders in the region and the world has seen India take a position of greater benevolence toward its people and its resources. Thus, India has declared that energy and food security are as important as military might in its national security plans.

India has been rattling its sabers toward China and Pakistan for fifty years. Disputes over its borders in the state of Jammu and Kashmir have been drawing significant resources and maintaining tension in New Delhi. India accuses Pakistan of harboring Islamic terrorists, some of whom it believes were responsible for the deadly bombings in Mumbai in 2006. Pakistan has made overtures to India that it would sue for peace if India recognizes Kashmir as an independent state.

Disaster Management

There's very little that India can do about preventing natural disasters like earthquakes and tsunamis. What the country can do is develop and implement a better system of responding to national emergencies. The Central and local government did a mediocre job of managing areas struck by recent disasters, largely due to the poor distribution of aid, food, and medical supplies. Fostered largely by the cultural bias against Dalits and Scheduled Tribes, it took an international intervention to see that everyone received access to help and assistance. India cannot afford another embarrassment like this.

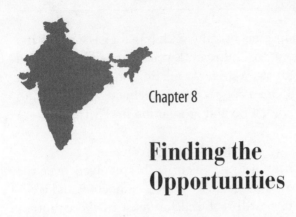

Chapter 8

Finding the
Opportunities

For firms new to working in the developing world, finding opportunities in the Indian boom will require some adjustments. It will consume more of your time and resources than you might imagine at first. Contrary to what you've been reading in most of the business magazines, there's no more gold on the streets of Mumbai than there was 100 years ago on the streets of New York City. So, where do you begin?

Well, I can sum it up by advising you to follow the money to the biggest cities, because that's where much of the action is taking place right now. Virtually all of India's growing middle class lives and works in and around the major city centers. That's where much of the new infrastructure is going in, where apartment complexes and shopping centers are being built, and where new office towers are reaching to the sky. Granted, 70 percent of the country is still rural—and wonderful things are also starting to happen there—but the best place for the U.S. businessperson to go searching is in the urban areas.

Depending on the nature of your business or service, there are several avenues that you can follow. These are discussed in the sections that follow. Although I do encourage you to especially study and reflect upon the first section (Personal Contacts) and the last section (Bribery and the FCPA) in the chapter, feel free to pick and choose those that might work best for you. Don't forget, regardless of the route you may decide to pursue, that the ever-changing Indian business regulations always apply, such as prohibitions on retailing unless you're offering a single brand.

Personal Contacts

Ask ten Indian entrepreneurs for their advice on the best way to uncover opportunities, and I'll bet that at least eight will reply, "Personal contacts." Based only on the numbers, the lion's share of business introductions and dealings are made through personal contacts.

This is not a big surprise as similar generalizations can be made about dealings here in the United States. However, in India the percentage is much higher, largely because most businesses are smaller and in the Unorganized Sector, where they're fairly invisible to most formal search services, and the average Indian's personal network stretches much farther than the average American's. Right now, many entrepreneurial Indians are traveling around major metropolitan areas in search of investment opportunities that they believe will be attractive to foreigners. Some of these fellows are speculators hoping to flip a business the way Americans flip houses. Others have been retained as agents for a fee or commission. Indian and U.S. investment firms also employ them.

Developing and leveraging contacts can be very time-consuming for foreigners, especially those with limited access to India. Unless you have already established solid relationships with upstanding Indian nationals you implicitly trust, such as attorneys, accountants, bank officers, or existing clients, I would recommend that you consider retaining an Indian firm or individual using an agent agreement.

There are several ways to find a reputable Indian agent. One is to work through industry/trade associations and chambers of commerce in the metropolitan area that interests you. For example, in Mumbai, I would go directly to the Maharashtra Economic Development Council, where I already have good contacts. If you're uneasy with this cold-call approach, then the best way for you to go is through the U.S. Commercial Service's International Partner Search (IPS) or Gold Key Service (GKS) programs. Both are fee-based and will require some upfront work on your part.

International Partner Search (IPS)

For small or new-to-export firms with limited resources, the IPS program can locate, screen, assess, and provide lists of prequalified agents familiar with the business sector in the city that you are interested in researching. At $500, IPS services are well worth the price because you don't have to leave the United States. IPS representatives in India also may be available to help you cull the lists down to a manageable size.

Gold Key Service (GKS)

For firms that are ready to sit down with potential agents, partners, and companies, or just feel the need for face-to-face interactions, the GKS program can facilitate meetings and site visits with prequalified businesspeople, government officials, and industry-specific associations. The GKS can act as your in-country escort, conduct confidential pre- and post-meeting briefings with your executives, and assist with travel and accommodation arrangements. The GKS is more expensive than the IPS because it offers much more in the way of hands-on services. The GKS is currently available in Ahmedabad, Bangalore, Chennai, Hyderabad, Kolkata, Mumbai, and New Delhi.

Trade Missions

Trade missions can be a good way to locate opportunities, but it's crucial that you go on the right one and for the correct reasons. While you are reading this book, there are airplanes crisscrossing the Atlantic Ocean and the Middle East carrying people to and from trade missions to India. One of these planes might be a U.S. Air Force C32A executive transport carrying the U.S. Assistant Secretary of State for South and Central Asia and CEOs of Halliburton, GE, and Microsoft to New Delhi. Another plane might be a Gulfstream carrying a small delegation of senior corporate officers or board members from several companies to a U.S.-India Business Council event in Hyderabad. A third might be ferrying several hundred delegates on a trade mission organized by the U.S.-based Chemical Manufacturers Association to a national fair in Mumbai sponsored by the Indian Chemical Council. A fourth could be taking a half-dozen Non-Resident Indians who own and operate tiny family businesses to a local trade mission sponsored by the Mumbai World Trade Center's chapter.

Which of these planes do you belong on? Clearly, there is no shortage of trade-related events in and about India that could be useful to you. The secret is to pick the one that will best serve your needs. This, however, is not an exact science, and you may find yourself settling for one that's somewhat imperfect. In that case, you need to be the final arbiter as to what you want to get from an event.

The first step when selecting a trade mission is to be realistic. Unless you are a high-level executive with a *Fortune* 100 company, it's unlikely that you'll be invited to or want to attend a U.S.-India Business Council event. These are policy-level forums and not viable sources for on-the-street information or contacts. On the other end of the spectrum, some local or state trade promotion groups may offer trade missions without being able to provide the necessary level of focus or insight on your specific product line or industry.

For example, a few years ago I was one of several expert speakers at an international business conference. That evening, at the official networking cocktail party, one of the other speakers struck up a conversation about his line of work, which was direct marketing in Asia. He then turned the discussion to how he had managed to secure a contract with a U.S.-based trade-promotion group to lead a trade mission to an Asian country he had spoken about that day—as an expert. As it finally turned out, he had never been to the country or even to the continent it was located on and was fishing for leads and information to help him pull it off! Perhaps an isolated incident, but needless to say, I'm not a fan of these off-the-cuff trade missions for that very reason. Remember, you'll pay about the same for a great one as you'll pay for a bad one.

The two best types to consider are trade missions sponsored by national industry associations and trade missions affiliated with or organized by U.S. government agencies. Hopefully, your firm is a member of one or more industry associations, so you'll be able to get on board as early as possible. The International Trade Administration of the U.S. Department of Commerce is a wonderful source of information on upcoming trade missions. These include those it is directly affiliated with, trade missions affiliated with other U.S. government departments and agencies, and trade missions from around the world that it believes have merit.

The next step in the selection process is to research the organization producing the event and ask them some hard and direct questions:

- **Is this the organization's first-ever trade mission, or are they seasoned veterans?** It's important to burrow a little deeper here. For example, an organization promoting its first overseas event should be wise enough to have hired a qualified and well-staffed event coordinator or conference producer to handle all the details. On the other hand, the seasoned veteran's Indian partner may have gotten a little lazy and might be offering what he can easily produce rather than what you may want, such as programs disproportionately full of side trips to the local temples and bazaars and laden with keynote speakers from low-level municipal departments. That's not an event I would consider attending.

- **Can the list of registered delegates be made available well in advance?** Organizers have a responsibility to protect the privacy of their customers, so you may be met with some resistance to this request. Be persistent; tell them you really don't need everyone's name. Ask for a head count of the confirmed attendees and a list of the companies they represent. This will enable you to gauge the event's interest among your business peers and give you a feel for how well your personal networking with other attendees may go. If the organizer still resists, you may want to consider taking your business elsewhere as it's likely the event will be a flop.

- **What is the cancellation policy?** Sometimes you may have to cancel at the last minute. Or if you find and commit to an interesting event shortly before it's scheduled to depart, subsequent research might show it's not the right event for you after all. Reputable organizations should be amenable to refunding all of your deposit, or at least all less a small processing fee, if you cancel within a reasonable amount of time. However, don't expect them to refund paid-up airline tickets or non-refundable hotel reservations. If the terms are unreasonable, it's probably best to walk away.

- **Who are the speakers at the event?** A trade mission may be part of a much larger event, such as an industry conference or annual meeting that has its own program of seminars, workshops, and keynote and dinner speakers. If you have time, try to find out a few things about some of the speakers. Is the consultant who is presenting on the future of the Indian economy a former U.S. Under-Secretary of State for Indian Economic Affairs? Yes? That's good. How about the team tapped to discuss transportation and infrastructure? If it's the local express-mail salesperson, you might want to use that time more effectively.

You should be able to make a good decision about the event once you have answered these questions to your satisfaction.

Contracting and Subcontracting

When it comes to business in India, contracting and subcontracting are wild cards. Most U.S. outsourcing to India for information technology (IT), business process outsourcing (BPO), software, and publication services has been in the forms of contracts. It's only recently that U.S. firms have actually begun establishing their own presence in India. The record suggests that India generally views contracting and subcontracting as the importing and exporting of human resources, which it is. Locating contract and subcontract services in India, then, is no different from looking for any other Indian exportable service.

Locating opportunities for contracting or subcontracting *into* India is a little different. At this stage in India's development, the options for U.S. contractors and subcontractors are largely limited to tenders from development agencies and development banks, although that will change as more and more foreign capital moves in. Much of the development money is finding its way into large infrastructure, energy, and real estate projects.

The first two are the exclusive territory of the Central and state governments and no private players, Indian or foreign, can legitimately offer the work. The World Bank Group and its affiliated regional development banks, the Export-Import Bank of the United States (Ex-Im Bank), the U.S. Agency for International Development (USAID), the Overseas Private Investment Corporation (OPIC), and other foreign development agencies finance projects in this field. Each of these has its own prequalification and procurement process, so your next step should be to directly contact all that you believe you are qualified to work for. Besides the development agencies, suppliers of unique equipment and services may have a need for contractor services. Turbine and large engine manufacturers are an example of this. It's important to keep in touch with U.S.-based vendors.

Subcontractors have more options, even though their product is more specialized, because they have many more potential customers (that is, prime contractors) to work for. Subcontractors also should establish relationships with the global and regional development agencies and banks. They're the ones doling out the contracts, so it's their stable of work and their schedule that you'll need to be aware of. Sometimes, contracts with U.S. development banks and agencies may go to a foreign (even Indian) prime contractor, but they'll certainly have significant set-asides for U.S. subcontracting and equipment. Also, they may provide your name and credentials to the contractors on their bid lists, or at the very least give you the necessary contact information to pursue the contractors yourself.

Besides projects driven by the global players, other municipal and private-sector opportunities from all across the board will present themselves at regular intervals. For example, many of India's business sectors are using contracts as vehicles to get the help they desperately need to upgrade equipment, add to supplier networks, maintain or upgrade infrastructure, establish educational and training facilities and resources, and do many other things we consider routine business-to-business activities in the States. Many of these contracts are between U.S. and Indian companies, while others are public-private partnerships, depending on the nature of the business.

One way to uncover these leads is to attend large-scale trade shows anywhere Indian companies are expected to be exhibiting in significant numbers. For example, over 300 Indian companies were in attendance at the 2006

Hannover Technology Fair, held annually in Germany. Can your product or service help them expand domestically or get exportable work? If so, you're in a great position to do business there.

Networking with Indian trade groups is also worthwhile for establishing a gateway into the country. For example, the Builders Association of India, headquartered in Mumbai, has ninety-seven operating centers throughout the country. Finally, don't rule out working overseas for an Indian company. Several Indian constructors have done work in Latin America on projects financed in part by U.S. or World Bank development resources.

Direct Selling and Direct Marketing

Direct selling and direct marketing of consumer and commercial products are two of the fastest-growing industries in India. In recent years, the market for direct selling in India topped $600 million and employed over 1.3 million people, based on data published by the World Federation of Direct Selling Associations. Based on U.S. Department of Commerce reports of industry estimates, there are over twenty direct-selling companies offering a nationwide presence, and over 100 have a significant local, urban presence.

Some of the best-known names operating in this sector as Indian corporations (that is, joint ventures or wholly owned subsidiaries) are Amway, Avon, Herbalife, Tupperware, and AMC cookware. Of these, the U.S. Department of Commerce puts Amway at the top, with over 200,000 distributors operating in over twenty-six cities. Many U.S. and foreign firms use direct selling and direct marketing because they are locked out of the retail sector by federal laws, although Indian retailers are beginning to turn to these methods, too.

Although included under a single heading, direct selling and direct marketing (indirect selling) are different. Direct selling refers to the face-to-face demonstrations and sales of products and services (consumer as well as commercial) by a product representative to an individual customer or to a group of customers. On the other hand, direct marketing or indirect selling does not require a face-to-face or person-to-person contact between the representative and the customer or buyer. Some common examples of direct marketing are bulk mail and catalogs, advertisements on Web sites, and newspaper inserts and flyers.

Here in the United States, we're all familiar with the quintessential example of direct selling, the Tupperware party. Those of us who are old enough also can remember the Fuller Brush man knocking on the front door every few months. Younger people are very familiar with Amway. In India, huge numbers of businesses and industries rely on direct selling to move products and services.

Both methods have merit and work in India, but each has its relative strengths and should be applied accordingly. It's likely that consumer products, such as home care, cosmetics, personal care, and nutritional supplements generate the bulk of their sales from direct selling, and commercial and business-to-business products generate most of theirs through direct marketing, such as from catalog sales.

Demographic trends are that younger, urban Indians are moving away from print media and into electronic media, where direct marketing is the only option. So, you should seriously consider buying advertising space on popular Web sites if your target market is younger. By the way, the Web is also the most popular place where urban professionals go looking for spouses.

Direct selling in India is lightly regulated, with only a minimum age requirement. Job-specific training of new hires is advisable to ensure uniformity and quality in the field. Turnover rates are high, as might be expected for a job with no required qualifications, and can be discouraging to new players in the market. Legislation specific to the roles and responsibilities of the industry is in the works, but it's not apparent if it will clear or blur the lines between direct selling and retailing.

The Central Government is concerned with protecting the rights of consumers as well as preventing mistreatment of the sales representatives. Any sales organization structured as a pyramid, Ponzi scheme, chain letter, or lottery—where entry fees or investments are required but sales are not—is illegal.

Indian laws recognize direct sellers as agents for the manufacturers or distributors, meaning they are not directly responsible for anything other than the sale itself. All matters pertaining to returns, repairs, warranties, and other claims are the responsibility of the manufacturer or distributor. Sales representatives are compensated with commissions on sales. In the case of multi-level marketing firms, compensation comes from the representative's own sales and sales from their network organization.

More information can be obtained from the Indian Direct Selling Association and the Direct Marketing Association: India. These organizations can provide industry reports on subjects like direct mail, telecommunications, credit cards, and publications. They also organize as well as represent their membership at regional seminars, training events, and conferences. It is interesting to note, *Reader's Digest* and Guthy-Renker are some of the members of the Direct Marketing Association: India, and Amway is a founding member of the Indian Direct Selling Association.

Franchising

Doing business as a franchise is a relatively new concept in India, although several U.S. hotel and food service firms got their start there in the early 1990s. It's likely that franchising would still be a minor industry had Indian marketers (and middle-class consumers) not become acutely aware of the power of branding. The Indian government estimates that the franchising sector has grown at average rates ranging from 20 percent to 30 percent compared to the national growth rate, which has averaged around 7 percent. Based on U.S. Department of Commerce reports, it is estimated that the number of franchisees in India is in the neighborhood of 50,000 units through contracts with up to 700 franchisors. The market exceeds $2 billion in annual sales. Some big-name Indian franchises are Apollo Hospitals, Archies, and MRF. Examples of U.S. firms with well-established franchise operations in India include the following:

- **Consumer products:** Disney Consumer Products, Tommy Hilfiger, and Office 1 Superstore
- **Car rental:** Avis, Budget, and Hertz
- **Food service:** Dunkin' Donuts, TGI Friday, Subway, and McDonald's
- **Hotels:** Best Western, Radisson, and Quality Inn

Other sectors with active growth in franchising include education, training, personal fitness, and courier services.

There are no franchise-specific regulations. However, all laws and regulations that pertain to the franchise's industry sector (such as single-branded retail or food) and the type of business arrangement (joint venture, subsidiary, and so on) must be complied with. These could include contracts; intellectual property, including trademark protection, copyright protection, and confidential business information; anti-monopoly and anti-competition; consumer protection; product liability; foreign exchange; labor; corporate and personal income taxes; real estate; and industry-specific state and local laws and regulations.

Many franchise arrangements in India take various forms of partnerships, especially between a franchisee and the owner or leaseholder of appropriate commercial retail space. The owner/leaseholder underwrites the startup and operating costs and shares in the profits. Obviously, choosing this route requires a great deal of knowledge about the financial stability and security of both the franchisee and the principals with the retail space. Sharing the same vision, goals, and work ethic are equally critical to long-term survival, as franchisees have been known to change the franchise in the retail space if revenues are not meeting projections.

The principal trade association in India is the Franchising Association of India, which is a member of the World Franchise Council. It has the resources to answer your questions and business relationships to help identify potential partners, financing, and business services.

Governments As Clients

Since India began privatizing its national industries, many former opportunities for government contracting are now handled by the private or private-public sector. Examples of sectors or industries that still remain under government control included defense, Air India, some banks, and Indian Railways.

India is not a signatory to the World Trade Organization Agreement on Government Procurement. The net result is that Indian government procurements and contracts are bid and rewarded in a shadow world where foreign firms rarely win anything unless they are the only legitimate source, such as military or civilian aircraft. Yet, most official Indian Web sites do link to current offerings. The Central Government's main Web site for reviewing and bidding on work is *www.tenders.gov.in*. Tenders may not appear on the specific Web site where you would logically expect to find them. One reason for this is the contracting agency might be different from the benefiting agency. A tender for work at Indian Railways may only appear on the Central Government Web site. Conversely, tenders that appear on the Indian Railways Web site may not appear on the Central Government Web site. Needless to say, if you're interested in pursuing direct contracting with Indian governments, you should visit all pertinent Web sites.

You're far more likely to uncover an opportunity with the U.S. government or another Organization for Economic Cooperation and Development (OECD) government working in India. All U.S. government contract opportunities above $25,000 are posted at *www.fedbizopps.gov*. Firms interested in opportunities for federal grants instead of contracts should visit *www.grants.gov*. The best way to find information on foreign government opportunities in India is to contact the U.S. Department of Commerce country desk for the country you're interested in contracting with.

NGOs As Clients

There are thousands of non-governmental organizations (NGOs) operating in India. These NGOs range in size from tiny one-person operations all the way up to the Indian representative of global organizations; they cover almost every subject and sector you can think of, from apple growing to zoology. Consistent with the U.N. Millennium Development Goals, the vast majority of NGOs in India are working in areas of sustainable development to address poverty and malnutrition, education, gender equality and empowerment of women, child mortality, maternal health, HIV/AIDS, environmental stability, and sustainable business and trade. As you can see, there are many options for opportunity here.

Most NGOs are funded by private organizations, government agencies, international agencies, and development agencies in amounts beginning at a few thousand dollars and heading upward. Here is a very small sample of agencies funding NGOs in India:

- Bill & Melinda Gates Foundation
- CARE International
- Citigroup Foundation

- Embassy of Japan
- European Union
- Ford Foundation
- Habitat for Humanity
- Indian Oil Foundation
- Lions Club
- MacArthur Foundation
- Rabo Bank
- Swiss Development Corporation
- USAID
- World Bank Group

There's no magic formula to finding opportunities in this sector, as it's mostly a matter of timing, data mining, and brute force. I would recommend that you do at least these two things:

1. Cultivate relationships with those funding organizations and agencies active in the sector you're interested or qualified to work in so they're aware of your presence and may even help steer you toward opportunities they become aware of.
2. Subscribe to as many relevant e-mail and snail-mail mailing lists as you can. These list owners often share their subscribers' contact information with like-minded organizations looking to publicize an event or even advertise requests for proposals and job openings. I've learned about opportunities in India funded by European agencies when their solicitation simply landed in my e-mail inbox, because my e-mail address had been loaned to an Indian NGO.

Bribery and the Foreign Corrupt Practices Act

You remember that old saying, "Fool me once, shame on you. Fool me twice, shame on me." Apparently, some

Indian elected officials have no shame, because getting caught in bribery stings has become a routine. As reported in the *International Herald Tribune*, Indian television stations have made sport of crafting scams they secretly videotape and then broadcast on the evening news to boost ratings. Recent back-to-back episodes have appeared on rival stations in which several members of parliament demanded kickbacks or accepted cash bribes from fictitious organizations to promote nonexistent development projects and to ask inane questions of the government while in session (a fairly common one). One MP was even caught in both of these stings! When viewers were polled about these and similar incidents, they were more surprised at the small amounts of the bribes than at the bribery, itself.

The main action these exposés seem to have triggered is an upswing in the sales of pocket-sized radio-frequency detectors, which alerts the wearer that a recording device is operating within fifteen feet. Even now, advertisements soliciting persons experienced in the art of "lubricating" top executives in banks have recently appeared in major newspapers. Are these ads real or just more stings? Well, it really doesn't matter, because their very presence implies that bribery is tightly woven into the fabric of everyday life in India.

American Sensitivity to Bribery and Corruption

In our time, Americans, too, have been sensitized by the political impacts of corruption. Events and activities leading up to Watergate have the highest profile and managed to bring down a sitting U.S. president. Yet we're still rank amateurs compared to India. In 1990, Airbus came under scrutiny amid allegations it had paid bribes to high-level officials to secure contracts for its aircraft over U.S. rival Boeing. *Hinduism Today* reported in 1997 that the accepted percentage of a major government contract necessary for the bribe was well known between the giver and recipient, and that corruption had come to mean the payoffs above and beyond what was normally given.

This isn't a recent trend. A 1987 arms scandal rocked the government of Rajiv Gandhi, who once commented that only 15 percent of what the government spends actually reaches the common man. His mother and predecessor as prime minister, Indira Gandhi, once dismissed criticism of corruption in India by remarking that corruption was a worldwide phenomenon. If so, how pervasive is it, and where does India rank?

The World's Watchdog on Corruption

Transparency International *(www.transparency.org)* is the top global watchdog keeping an eye on corruption. The German-based organization surveys experts for their opinions and uses this composite information to assess and quantify the level of corruption in a country's business practices over the past two years. In actuality, it's the subsidiaries of multinational corporations that are being ranked by the experts.

During the most recent two-year period, India is perceived to have improved its anti-corruption practices. Interestingly, the United States is perceived to have slipped a little, despite having its very own punitive laws against bribery in international business.

The 2006 Corruption Perceptions Index scores 163 countries on a scale from 10 (perfect) to 0 (worst). Although major corruption scandals do still appear in high-ranking countries, industrialized countries generally score highly in the index while failed states and historically underdeveloped states score poorly. According to Transparency International, data in the 2006 index points to a strong correlation between corruption and poverty, with a concentration of impoverished states at the bottom of the ranking.

Perceived Corruption in Selected Countries

Country Rank	Country	Score
1	Finland	9.6
1	New Zealand	9.6
7	Switzerland	9.1
9	Australia	8.7
11	United Kingdom	8.6
15	Hong Kong	8.3
17	Japan	7.6
20	United States	7.3
42	Mauritius	5.1
70	India	3.3
70	China	3.3
70	Brazil	3.3
70	Mexico	3.3
111	Vietnam	2.6
121	Russia	2.5
130	Indonesia	2.4
142	Pakistan	2.2
163	Haiti	1.8

Source: Transparency International—2006 Corruption Perceptions Index

U.S. Efforts to Subvert Corrupt Business Practices

The United States has been a pioneer in the fight against corruptive practices in business. The Foreign Corrupt Practices Act (FCPA) took effect in 1977 after U.S. government investigations related to Watergate showed over 400 U.S. companies had paid over $300 million in bribes to foreign officials and politicians.

When passed, the FCPA was intended to stop bribery and restore public confidence in the integrity of the U.S. business system. In 1998, the act was amended to reflect ratification of the OECD Anti-Bribery Convention, of which the U.S. was the principal initiator. The act was broadened to apply to foreign firms and persons who act corruptly.

This last part is important because many businesses are not familiar with the OECD Anti-Bribery Convention and the ramifications of the 1998 FCPA amendments. It also prohibits corrupt payments through third-party intermediaries. Its impact has been felt by corporations in the form of fines and debarment from business with the U.S. government and by those corporate officers and employees who have been given prison terms for their roles. The federal government has brought more FCPA cases in 2004 and 2005 than in the prior twenty-six years combined.

The antibribery provisions of the FCPA make it illegal for a U.S. person and certain foreign issuers of securities to make a corrupt payment to a foreign official for retaining or obtaining business. The antibribery provisions define who is affected, what corrupted intents are, what constitutes a payment, who a recipient is, and the business purpose test, which extends the prohibition to persons other than foreign government or government-agency officials. The following are some exceptions to what constitutes a bribe:

- Grease payments to lower-level officials to expedite or facilitate performance of routine government actions
- Payments that are legal under the written laws of the host country
- Payments for bona fide expenditures, such as travel or lodging related to a product demonstration or for performing a contract

Like most other U.S. laws, however, there are some gray areas, and it's best to err on the side of caution. Contact the U.S. Securities and Exchange Commission and U.S. Department of Justice for more information and guidance.

Chapter 9

Establishing a Presence in India

There are many ways to gain a foothold in the Indian economy, such as:

- Investing hard cash into an ongoing business, either directly or through capital markets and portfolios
- Purchasing part or all of an Indian company's assets
- Licensing a product to an Indian company
- Opening a franchise of a familiar U.S. business
- Establishing a foreign technology collaboration agreement
- Establishing ventures in Export Oriented Units (EOU), Special Economic Zones (SEZ), and Technology Parks (as discussed on page 175)

Obviously, one also can envision many possible combinations and variations on these. The size of an investment is carefully controlled by law and varies from sector to sector. Keep an eye on these restrictions because they may change without much advance warning. In the past, when Indian industry was still generally closed to foreigners, Indian companies formed subsidiaries in Mauritius solely for the purpose of establishing joint ventures with foreign partners. It worked reasonably well for the parties involved, and sophisticated investors may be keeping this door open.

Legal Framework

Like Great Britain, India is a common-law country with a constitution that guarantees property rights. There are laws that cover all major areas pertinent to business as well as regulations and policies to effect their implementation. Matters of law related to property and personal rights are decided in the courts. Some of the most significant laws affecting foreign investment in India and the year of their enactment are:

- Indian Contract Act, 1872
- Negotiable Instruments Act, 1881
- Trade Unions Act, 1926
- Sales of Goods Act, 1930
- Partnership Act, 1932
- Industrial Disputes Act, 1947
- Factories Act, 1948
- Emblems and Names Act, 1950
- Industries Act, 1951
- Companies Act, 1956
- Copyright Act, 1957
- Trade and Merchandise Mart Act, 1958
- Income Tax Act, 1961
- Customs Act, 1962
- Monopolies and Restrictive Trade Practices Act, 1969
- Consumer Protection Act, 1986
- Benami Transactions (Prohibitions) Act, 1988
- Foreign Trade (Development and Regulation) Act, 1992
- Securities and Exchange Board of India Act, 1992
- Trade Marks Act, 1999
- Information Technology Act, 2000
- Competition Act, 2002
- Companies Amendment Act, 2006

Along with policies issued by the Central Government, the major laws affecting business activities are the Foreign Trade (Development and Regulation) Act, the Industries Act, the Companies Act, and the Monopolies and Restrictive Trade Practices Act. In addition to these statutes there are regular changes to the New Industrial Policy of 1991, which was the policy that liberated the Indian economy after national bankruptcy was narrowly averted.

Gaining a Foothold

India offers an investor the opportunity to acquire as much as 100 percent of an enterprise, depending on a number of factors related to the business sector or business activity. The main government gateways for investment are the Reserve Bank of India, India's Ministry of Industry, and India's Ministry of Finance, whose gatekeeper is a high-level agency called the Foreign Investment Promotion Board (FIPB). The FIPB clears foreign proposals for investments in India, and its members include ministry-level officials from the Ministries of Commerce and Industries and the Ministry of External Affairs. Within the Ministry of Industry, the Secretaries for Industrial Assistance (SIA) actually handles proposals and applications, reviewing and forwarding them to the FIPB. SIA also is the government's resource center and government-interface that investors can work with to prepare their proposals and applications. Applications also can be made with overseas Indian missions.

Prior approvals by the government (that is, the FIPB) and the Reserve Bank of India is usually required for all investments. Fortunately, there are a fast-track method called the Automatic Route for approving a subset of business investments under which the investors are not required to obtain prior approval from the government or Reserve Bank of India. On the Automatic Route, investors in qualifying business sectors only need to notify the regional branch of the Reserve Bank of India within thirty days of their deposit and to file all required documents with that office within thirty days of issuing shares to foreign investors.

Sector Breakdown

Investment in some business sectors cannot be done using the Automatic Route and does require prior approval by the Central Government, Reserve Bank of India, and possibly the state government. These include:

- Products that require an industrial license.
- Acquisition of shares in an existing Indian company.
- Manufacture in the tobacco sector.
- Manufacture of electronic, aerospace, and defense equipment.
- Manufacture of products specifically reserved for the Small-Scale Sector (if the intent is to acquire more than 24 percent of the concern).
- Increased investment in a business in the financial or technical sector where the investor already has an interest (that is, anti-monopoly).
- All investments falling outside specific business-sector policies or caps.

The American businessperson needs to be aware that several business sectors, both private and government, are still partially or completely closed to direct investment:

- Atomic energy
- Betting
- Gambling
- Lottery
- Retail (except single-branded product retailing)

The retail sector is an interesting case. Despite the prohibition on direct ownership, foreign retailers have carved a firm toehold in the Indian consumer sector. They have done this by establishing wholesale distributorships that directly provide products to Indian retailers, who mimic their suppliers' business practices in the United States and Europe.

Other sectors are conditionally open, with various restrictions on the percentage of ownership and control allowed for foreign investors. Be aware that these rules frequently change, so thorough due diligence is advised. Here are a few selected examples of allowable investments (some with conditions):

- **100 percent allowed:** Development of new airports; coal exploration and mining; trading certain types of goods and services; parcel courier services; non-banking finance; power trading; alcohol, cigars, and cigarettes
- **Up to 74 percent allowed:** Redevelopment of existing airports; private-sector banking; satellite communications; providing Internet access and services
- **Up to 49 percent allowed:** Cable television; personal telecommunications services; domestic air transportation; infrastructure and services; and asset reconstruction
- **Up to 26 percent allowed:** FM radio; print media; defense industries; insurance; petroleum and natural gas

In addition to these reservations and constraints, all the typical clearances and approvals familiar to U.S. companies, such as construction and environmental permits, acquiring land and water rights, connecting to utilities, hiring employees, and contracting services will need to be addressed.

Small-Scale Industries

The business sector with the greatest variety and number of players is the Small-Scale Sector, which logically consists of small-scale industries (SSI). India's Ministry of

Small–Scale Industries oversees this, the fastest-growing sector in the country. The SSI accounts for over a third of the nation's exports and is the one that India is pinning its hopes on for the economic future of the majority of the people.

By definition, a small–scale business has invested no more than 50 million rupees in its capital plant and machinery, can manufacture any item, and is not restricted as to where it can operate. The size of a small business has been creeping upward, probably to offset inflation concerns as well as protect more of the economy from outside factors. The Central Government recognizes five legally legitimate types of SSI businesses:

- Small Scale Industrial Undertakings
- Ancillary Industrial Undertakings
- Tiny Enterprise
- Women Entrepreneur
- Small Scale Service and Business (industry related) Enterprises

Foreign investments in SSI businesses are capped at 24 percent. Care must be taken not to exceed this amount. Otherwise, strict licensing requirements kick in, and many of the incentives, exemptions, and services the government provides to SSI would no longer be available to the business. Within India's Ministry of Small-Scale Industries, the Small Industries Development Organization (SIDO) is tasked with providing hands-on assistance, guidance, and training to India's vast number of small businesses.

Industrial Licensing

Licensing a product or service is still the cleanest and cheapest way of doing business in India. Regardless of how simple or complex the product is, there still is a wealth of interest on the part of Indian companies in being able to skip over research and development and to start churning out profitable goods, especially for export. Many U.S. businesses got their first opportunity in India by licensing and have been successful at not only staying in-country but expanding into new areas as the Central Government opened the investment doors. Fortunately, the number and range of business sectors requiring licenses has shrunk, allowing U.S. companies to enter many Indian markets without delay.

Licensing Requirements

Currently, an industrial license is required in the following cases:

- For manufacture of any item reserved for the Small-Scale Sector.
- Where location-specific restrictions are in place.
- For industries where compulsory licensing is a logical requirement, such as for national security or protection of public health and the environment.

If a business determines that it is exempt from licensing requirements, it must file an Industrial Entrepreneur Memorandum (IEM) with the government. Obviously, the IEM would become null and void if the business decided to begin manufacturing products that required licenses.

To support the millions of Indians who work in the Small-Scale Sector, the Central Government has set aside specific products that only the Small-Scale Sector can produce. This list changes often, so it's best to consult government guidance as to what is allowable and what is not. A business not classified as small-scale but wishing to manufacture any of these set-aside products must obtain an industrial license and commit to export at least 50 percent of its production before beginning operations.

In the special case of a successful small business outgrowing it's small-scale exemption, the Central Government offers a Carry On Business License that allows the firm to continue production at a rate based on its maximum output during the three preceeding years without having to begin exporting the product and adversely impact its domestic customer base. However, an industrial license would be required if the business grows further and exceeds the limits specified in its Carry On Business License. Obviously, creativity is rewarded in the Small-Scale Sector.

Although businesses are not restricted from operating throughout India, the Central Government does require a business to obtain a license if it wishes to operate in or near highly populated urban areas. This applies if the business is to be located within fifteen miles of the limits of the Standard Urban Area of India's major cities having populations of at least 1 million in 1991. Standard Urban Area is defined as an area with a town of at least 50,000 people with continuous growth around it encompassing a number of smaller towns and rural settlements and with the possibility of becoming urban in the future.

Some examples are the greater metropolitan areas around Ahmedababd, Bangalore, Bhopal, Chennai, Coimbatore, Delhi, Indore, Kolkata, and Mumbai. In states like Maharashtra, where Greater Mumbai lies, the majority of the state's land area falls within the limits of the standard urban area. This could mean that a business wishing to set up practically anywhere in Maharashtra may need a license to operate.

Fortunately, the Central Government has created exemptions from licensing within these geographic areas in the following situations: for so-called nonpolluting industries, such as electronics, computer software, printing, or other businesses given that definition, and for businesses to be located in an area designated as an industrial area by the government before July 25, 1991.

The Central Government has made licensing a compulsory requirement for the following business sectors:

- Distilling and brewing alcoholic beverages.
- Manufacturing cigars, cigarettes, and tobacco substitutes.
- Manufacturing all types of electronic, aerospace, and defense equipment.
- Manufacturing industrial explosives.
- Manufacturing specific highly hazardous chemicals.

It's possible that more industries and sectors will be added to this list in the future as India's regulatory systems mature.

Technology Collaborations

High-profile Indians are very proud of their country's success in information technology and business process operations, and they are looking toward all kinds of research and development (scientific, financial, and so on) to fuel the next bump in growth. Yet India has largely emerged into the modern world carried on the back of imported technology, and its appetite for this industry-creating magic pill hasn't diminished a bit. The Central Government strongly encourages foreign technology collaborations and allows payments for technical know-how, designs, drawings, and engineering services. However, certain actions and services, such as hiring foreigners, exporting Indian technical personnel, and out-of-country testing of Indian products and services are not allowed in technology collaborations. These, and similar actions, are regulated by the Reserve Bank of India under other trade-related rules.

Royalties are calculated on the price of the product, less deductions for costs of specific components. This can be tricky, so tread lightly when looking for opportunities in this arena. Payment and compensation for technology transfers are capped as follows:

- Lump-sum payments cannot exceed $2 million.
- Royalties on in-country sales are capped at 5 percent (net of taxes, etc.).
- Royalties on export sales are capped at 8 percent (net of taxes, etc.).

Trademarks and Brand Names

Business arrangements in which trademarks and brand names are licensed or franchised to Indian companies can become quite intricate and convoluted. For example, the cultural and culinary differences between the United States and India may prompt in-country franchisees to create their own versions of U.S.-branded consumer products, especially food and drink. In instances like this, who will own the rights to the new product? Will a reverse license be required? How will royalties be determined? You get the picture. Fortunately, India is fairly safe with respect to protection of most forms of intellectual property, with the exceptions of copyright enforcement and pharmaceutical manufacture, and is certainly better than Brazil, China, or Russia.

India allows payments of royalties for the use of trademarks and brand names in two ways: when used in standalone arrangements; and when used as part of a technology transfer. For standalone arrangements, payments of royalties are capped at 2 percent of net sales on exports and 1 percent on in-country net sales. When used as part of a technology transfer, payments of royalties on use of trademarks and brand names are included in the overall royalties paid on sales of the technology; that is, separate royalties for trademarks, brand names, and technology sales are not allowed.

Environmental Clearances

India has some of the worst air- and water-pollution problems in the world. Visitors to the Delhi region are routinely assaulted by smog produced from motor vehicles and industry. Within India, twenty-four geographic areas have been designated for priority action, which means things are in desperate straits. Due to this, the government of India is very sensitive to the need to control pollution and protect public health and the environment while enabling economic development to expand. Much of the day-to-day work in environmental management, such as conducting permit-related inspections, is done by state agencies. New projects of significant size are required to produce an Environmental Impact Assessment (EIA) although pipeline construction is one that is exempt from this requirement.

Currently, thirty-one industry classifications require one or more permits or approved EIAs before they are allowed to begin construction or operate a facility. Sectors and industries like fossil-fuel–fired power plants, cement manufacture, petroleum refining, petrochemical production, pulp and paper manufacture, dyestuff and fertilizer production, and pharmaceutical manufacture are just some examples of the businesses affected by statutory requirements for environmental clearances.

The size of the venture does play a role in whether clearances will be necessary. Investment projects smaller than 1 billion rupees may not be required to obtain clearances unless they are in certain industries or within specific geographic regions. Most of these industries are familiar to the U.S. investor, such as pesticides, bulk pharmaceuticals, asbestos (mining/refining) and asbestos products, mining and metal foundries, distilleries, electroplating, dyes and dyestuffs, certain types of tourism projects, and road surfacing and paving in the Himalayas. Also, areas considered ecologically fragile, such as coastal areas, the Aravalli Range, and the Doon Valley, have their own guidelines.

Non-Resident Indians and Persons of Indian Origin

Like everything else in India, opportunities and restrictions are in a constant state of flux. Although the foreign money for a joint venture or go-it-alone effort may be coming from outside India, the Central Government does differentiate between investors. For years, foreigners and Indian nationals and their overseas relatives were forbidden to invest in Indian ventures from outside the country. Much of that has changed, and current restrictions are minimal.

A Non-Resident Indian (NRI) is an Indian citizen who leaves the country for an extended period of time for employment or to conduct business and who draws his or her income from out-of-county work. A Person of Indian Origin (PIO) is a citizen of any country, other than Pakistan or Bangladesh, who has ever held an Indian passport; was, or had either a parent or grandparent who was a citizen of India by virtue of the Constitution; or is the spouse of an Indian citizen. India's most famous PIO is Sonia Gandhi, President of the Indian National Congress and the widow of Rajiv Gandhi.

Foreigners, NRIs, and PIOs are held to slightly different standards when it comes to putting their money on the table as well as taking it back out of the country. Both NRIs and PIOs directly can invest cash into a company's capital. However, there are constraints on the sectors available for investment, such as any agricultural/plantation or real estate business, as well as repatriation of the funds outside of India. One way around this is to invest in sole proprietorships or partnerships approved by India's Department of Economic Affairs and the Reserve Bank of India.

India also has specific guidelines and prohibitions for the handling of equity shares between and among foreign investors and foreign employees. These are administered by the Reserve Bank of India, the Securities and Exchange Board of India (SEBI), and applicable or appropriate parts of the Substantial Acquisition of Shares and Takeovers Regulations of 1997 administer these, although some transfers are allowed under the Automatic Route.

Indian corporations, with prior approval by the government and the Reserve Bank of India, can raise virtually unlimited capital from the United States or other trading-partner countries for any purpose other than investing in real estate or Indian stocks by issuing American Depository Receipts (ADR), where applicable, or Global Depository Receipts (GDR). Also, Indian corporations can issue Foreign Currency Convertible Bonds (FCCB) in an amount up to $50 million using the Automatic Route and up to $100 million with approval from the Reserve Bank of India. Prior permission from the government is required for bond issues above $100 million. Bond issues must conform to all external commercial borrowing (end use) regulations. Up to 25 percent of the bond proceeds can be used for general restructuring of the corporation. Preference shares for the purpose of acquiring equity are allowed, although their issue, duration, and dividend are tightly controlled by government regulations and agencies. Current information can be obtained from the Government of India's Web site (*www.indian.gov.in*).

Deciding on the Business and Business Alliance

Every few weeks, one experiences a new or inventive way to get a business started in India. For a long time, the only route open to foreign investors with an eye on an Indian presence was to license their products or technologies to Indian firms, who would do all the in-country manufacturing, distributing, and marketing for compensation from the licensor through royalties or by other means. Over time, as more and more sectors opened to foreign ownership, the licensors acquired part, or all, of the licensee or formed joint ventures with in-country strategic partners.

There are two principal paths by which a foreign company or NRI can do business in India: as an incorporated Indian company or as a Foreign company. These aren't much different from what Americans are familiar with, except that India's foreign direct investment policies put specific controls and constraints on what one can and cannot do.

Conducting business in India without forming an incorporated Indian company is how the majority of Americans have succeeded to date. Businesses that can satisfactorily function through Branch Offices or Project Offices have largely been successful in gaining a foothold in the Indian economy.

There is a broad push on the part of the Indian government to: grow the more mature Export Oriented Units scheme, with its hundreds of locations throughout the country; establish Special Economic Zones in areas with reasonable access to the large seaports, where India offers the foreign business an option to establish a Branch Office on a standalone basis; and other sector-specific technology-park schemes. Furthermore, if an in-country marketing or a promotional presence is all that's necessary for a firm to get started, then India offers the options of establishing Liaison Offices or Representative Offices.

Forming the Indian Corporation

The safest and most logical way to establish an Indian company is to incorporate in India. Incorporating in India enables a foreign entity to form joint ventures with qualified parties or to form or acquire a wholly owned subsidiary of a qualified ongoing Indian business. It also provides a tax structure that usually is more attractive than other, less committed options.

The Companies Act, the Companies Amendment Act, and several bills related to specific activities govern the incorporation of a company in India. As in the United States, there are several options:

- **Private company:** In India, doing business as a private company offers some advantages. A private company can restrict the shareholder's right to transfer shares, can limit the number of its shareholders (not including its employees or former shareholders) to a maximum of fifty, does not offer invitations of investment to the public, cannot invite or accept deposits from anyone other than its shareholders, directors, or their relatives, and must demonstrate access to capital of 1 million rupees.

- **Public company:** A public company must have at least seven shareholders and at least three directors; hold corporate meetings on a regular schedule; obtain approval by the Central Government for the management it wishes to appoint; either publish a prospectus or file an acceptable and appropriate statement (in lieu of a prospectus); and demonstrate access to capital of 5 million rupees.

- **Private Limited Company (PLC):** A Private Limited Company can be formed by converting another business structure, such as an existing partnership or sole proprietorship or by simply incorporating as a PLC.

Principal Steps You'll Take

The incorporation process is fairly straightforward but can take longer than one might expect it should. In theory, this procedure can be initiated online from the United States by visiting India's Ministry of Corporate Affairs Web site (*www.mca.gov.in*), but I highly discourage doing it this way unless you are experienced at opening businesses in India. I also strongly encourage anyone considering incorporating a business in India to work very closely with the regional government offices during every step of the process—as the saying goes, "Measure twice, cut once." The principal components for incorporation are as follows:

- **Company name:** Select up to six unique names for the company (the desired name and five alternates, in case the desired name is not accepted by the government), and be sure to include the type of business in the name. (Have you ever wondered why Indian business names leave no doubt about what they do?) Check with the Central Government's guidelines and confirm that the naming is done in accordance with the Emblems and Names (Prevention of Improper Use) Act of 1950. Confirm that the proposed names are reasonably dissimilar to extant business names. Complete the proper form and submit it along with a filing fee to the appropriate Registrar of Companies office (for example, in the state or union territory in which the company will be registered to conduct business).

- **Memorandum of Association:** In India, a company's charter is called the Memorandum of Association (MoA), which legally defines the business. The MoA identifies the company's name; the state or union territory where it is registered; its principal business objectives; its members' personal liability (that is, officers, owners); and authorized capital. The MoA must be notarized before it can be considered legally valid.

- **Articles of Association:** The Articles of Association (AoA) identify the company's operations, internal lines of authority and responsibility, and how it will conduct business. Furthermore, the AoA spells out all the company's by-laws, rules, and regulations and must be fully subordinate to the MoA. Relationships between the company and its members are presented, and each is fully bound by the AoA. For a private company, the AoA also must be notarized for the company to be legally valid.

- **Registration:** Registering the company is fairly straightforward. Documents and information that the regional Registrar of Companies may be looking for include confirmation that the chosen name is available; the MoA; the AoA; all agreements between the company and its future directors and top managers;

evidence that all necessary registration and filing fees have been paid; and a declaration of compliance with all applicable, relevant, and appropriate regulations (such as the Companies Act).

Once all the hurdles are overcome, the Registrar of Companies will issue a Certificate of Incorporation, making the business a fully legal entity and ready to do business in accordance with its documents. If it is a public company, then a Certificate of Commencement of Business (known as the Trading Certificate) must be obtained before business affairs can be conducted. Once registered and with trading certificate in hand, the corporation can begin to raise capital and get down to the business of making money.

Setting Up the Alliance

Before India began opening its markets to foreign products and services, licensing agreements with Indian companies were the only real way to gain an entry. When business sectors began to open, many foreign firms acquired as much of the in-country manufacturing and distribution of their product as they could. Early on in the process, foreign investment was highly controlled, and the majority of the opportunities were only for non-controlling parts of companies. The net results of this are that most foreign acquisitions have resulted in corporate joint ventures with one or more Indian partners and that joint ventures have become the preferred way of entering the market.

Forming Joint Ventures

Joint ventures in India can be set up the same as any domestic Indian corporation; there are no special laws that pertain to joint ventures. Joint ventures are typically formed in one of three ways:

- When two parties form a brand-new company.
- When one party sells its business to the new joint venture for equity and the other acquires the remaining equity in the joint venture for cash.
- When one party acquires part of an existing business for cash to form the joint venture.

To initiate a joint venture, the two parties typically draft and co-sign a Memorandum of Understanding or a letter of intent that summarizes the basis of the intended agreement.

All joint ventures involving a foreigner or NRI require government approval. This approval may come from the Reserve Bank of India, the FIPB, or the Secretariat for Industrial Approvals.

If the Automatic Route covers the joint venture, then approval from the Reserve Bank of India is required. If the business sector in which the joint venture will operate is a special case not covered by the Automatic Route, then the formal process for application and approval through the FIPB must be followed. The list of business sectors covered by one or the other changes frequently, so it always is prudent to check for current information.

Forming a Project or Branch Office

Project and site offices to support and manage specific projects, such as construction and engineering, are easy to establish and operate. Permission to open a temporary project office comes from the Reserve Bank of India and is awarded contingent on the office's carrying on only those activities it was established to do for that project. Profits realized from the project can be remitted out of India at completion.

Branch offices are typically established to support and manage foreign, not in-country, manufacturing and trade activities. One classic example of a branch office is an office set up in India by a foreign airline or shipper to handle the business of carrying passengers and transporting cargo to and from India's major cities and commercial cargo and container ports. India allows foreign companies to establish branch offices for the following purposes:

- Importing and exporting goods
- Serving as in-country representation
- Acting as sales and purchasing agents
- Providing technical support for its products
- Promoting collaborations between itself and Indian companies
- Conducting research, professional, and consulting services
- Providing IT services and developing software

Branch offices are not allowed to manufacture or process, either directly or indirectly. Foreign companies can use their branch offices to contract manufacturing from an Indian company, but they are not permitted to carry out manufacturing on their own. Foreign companies interested in setting up a branch office must contact the regional offices of the Reserve Bank of India.

A relatively new and special class of branch office is one established on a standalone basis in a Special Economic Zone. These branch offices are restricted to conducting business activities only within the Special Economic Zone, even if its parent company has a presence elsewhere in India. It is an isolated business entity. Special Economic Zones are discussed in greater detail in the following section.

Export Oriented Units, Special Economic Zones, and Technology Parks

The government of India made the strategic decision to promote exports as a means of alleviating negative impacts on its balance of trade. Its export-and-import policy is focused on sustaining growth in exports and creates several incentives for investing in businesses in these sectors.

Unfortunately, the World Trade Organization prohibits export incentives. These usually take the form of tax breaks on investment income, and India is required to phase out these breaks. To get around these constraints, India has decided to pursue the path of tax-free exporting, which the World Trade Organization allows, by creating export-promotion schemes that ensure imports as well as finished products are made tax-free.

There are two ways that an investor can take advantage of this, either by completely isolating export production units from domestic production units or by providing domestic production units with tax-free inputs. Both of these can be implemented, with a few case-specific restrictions, by using one or more of the following schemes:

- Export Oriented Unit (EOU)
- Special Economic Zone (SEZ)
- Software Technology Park (STP)
- Electronics Hardware Technology Park (EHTP)
- Biotechnology Park (BTP)

All of these schemes are governed by different rules and granted different benefits.

The EOU concept has been around for a while and is successfully working throughout India. An EOU is an industrial company that exports its entire production and enjoys reduced or no duty and income taxes. The SEZ, a relatively new concept, is regarded as foreign territory for the purpose of duties and taxes and is not regulated by customs authorities. Many are converted Export Processing Zones (EPZ). The various technology parks are basically special-product versions of the broader EOU/SEZ. Technology parks can be set up within an EOU, an SEZ, or at a location designated for them by the government.

All offer some form of tax benefit or relief. Here are some of the highlights:

- An EOU is a standalone business.
- Over 300 locations are available throughout India for setting up an EOU, and estimates are that nearly 2,500 are currently in operation.
- An EOU can be set up within an existing manufacturing facility, as long as it's isolated from the domestic-production operation, and administrative costs can be shared.
- An EOU can easily be converted to a domestic tariff area.
- SEZs are located in areas specifically developed for them, which are generally near one of the country's major ports or points of exportation (Kandla, Mumbai, Cochin, Kolkata, Chennai, and Surat).
- 100 percent equity positions are allowed, except for those sectors requiring licensing or with caps on foreign investment.
- Sales are allowed to in-country domestic tariff areas.
- A business in an SEZ is tax exempt at its inception and incurs reduced tax liabilities over a seven-year period.
- SEZ units are allowed to carry forward operating losses for eight years.
- A business in an SEZ cannot be converted to a domestic tariff area without physically moving out of the SEZ.

The tax incentives, investment constraints, and other financial issues change at least annually, if not more frequently. A business should consider investing in an EOU/SEZ when a high percentage of raw materials or capital goods is imported and the final intention is to export all or most of the products. Indian businesses wishing to export their entire production of goods and services, but not to do trading, may be set up under the EOU/SEZ scheme or one of the sector-specific technology parks.

Exports are generally open to all manufactured goods, including repair, remaking, reengineering, and rendering of services, except for those specifically prohibited or conditionally restricted items and services, and conversion of the business from one to the other is allowable. EOUs operate in accordance with Central Government regulations and are not bound by state or union territory trading regimes.

Forming Representative Offices or Liaison Offices

Concerns about financial, personnel, intellectual property, or the partial or complete restrictions that are still in place in many business sectors, may cause foreign companies to delay their formal entry into the Indian marketplace until some time in the future. Yet having some type of presence in India to keep a finger on the pulse of the business activity is desirable. In cases like these, India offers the foreign or NRI business the opportunity to operate a representative or liaison office.

The activities of this office are entirely restricted to marketing and sales support, identifying business opportunities, and responding to queries for information about its services or products. It can facilitate collaborations between Indian companies and its parent company as well as carry on the promotion of exporting and importing. Representative and liaison offices are entirely dependent on their parent company for financial support and survival; they are not allowed to conduct any commercial activity or generate any income.

Identifying Partners, Agents, and Distributors

On the whole, I feel that India is reasonably sophisticated in terms of finding and developing solid business contacts who can advise and guide you through its changing landscape. Or, if taking a conservative approach suits your firm better, then beginning your search stateside is quite feasible and should yield useful results.

There is no shortage of people ready and willing to help foreigners get their businesses started. Depending on who you are and the firm you represent, these all-too-willing facilitators will range from the president of one of India's largest and most successful companies to the friend of the cousin of the fellow who waits on tables at the local Indian restaurant. If *caveat emptor* ever applied to guidance on penetrating a new market, this is the place—and stay away from singleton operators.

The first things you should evaluate are the firm's reputation and standing, marketing strength, industry expertise, financial capacity, willingness to invest, and credit rating. The firm should be willing to work on standard business terms for delivery and payment and should be capable of offering first-class showroom and promotional facilities. You should determine the firm's ability to move goods to markets and its marketing capabilities throughout the country or region you're interested in. The best place to begin the search is with U.S. and Indian government agencies.

U.S. Government Agencies

Within the U.S. federal government, several agencies are tasked with promoting exports and trade, especially to emerging markets and countries, such as India, with which the United States has cooperative agreements. These agencies and their overseas representatives are ready, willing, and able to point investors in the direction of many comprehensive resources, including demographic data, financing, lists of potential customers, leads to agents, distributors and consultants, and potential and legitimate joint-venture partners.

The International Trade Administration (ITA) of the U.S. Department of Commerce is the federal government's flagship agency for foreign trade. The role of the ITA is to help exporters focus their products, financing, market assembly, and logistics on the specific country or region they're interested in penetrating. Your first stop there should be the country desk officer for India.

The U.S. Commercial Service is the trade-promotion arm of the ITA. It currently operates offices in seven key Indian cities and offers the fee-based Gold Key Service (described on page 140), which can provide customized market and industry briefings, market research, in-country meetings with prospective trade partners, and help with travel, accommodations, and clerical support when necessary.

The U.S. Trade and Development Agency promotes commercial and public-private partnerships focused on industries and regions. U.S. companies are often partners in these efforts and are a good source of information and leads.

Other agencies whose primary missions may not be trade promotion nevertheless should have extensive contacts in India. Examples of these are the Overseas Private Investment Corporation (OPIC), the U.S. Department of State's Foreign Service, and the U.S. Agency for International Development.

State and Local Trade Promotion Groups

Interestingly, here in the United States our states and even larger port cities maintain their own trade development agencies and export assistance services—all paid for by sales and income taxes. Many are not country specific, but some do fund one or two in-country representatives, even in India. I'm not a big fan of these groups. Their services are fairly limited, their in-country representatives are often part-timers without access to the big-hitters, and they frequently interface with the same federal services that you can access yourself.

American Chamber of Commerce

The American Chamber of Commerce in India (AMCHAM-India) is an association of American business organizations in India. Based in New Delhi, AMCHAM-India offers an organized forum where U.S. businesses can share their experiences and views. It tracks timely country-specific and regional developments in politics, the economy, and business that are of interest to the U.S. investor. Through its five regional chapters in Bangalore, Chennai, Hyderabad, Kolkata, and Mumbai, AMCHAM-India strives to network U.S. and Indian businesses at a very personal and functional level. A visit to the regional AMCHAM-India office would be a good idea the next time you're in India.

Embassy of India and the Consulate General of India

Here in the United States, the official gateways to India are the Embassy of India in Washington, D.C., and the Consulate General of India with offices in New York, Chicago, Houston, and San Francisco. Both of these largely serve diplomatic liaison roles, but they also provide a good source of socioeconomic and political information about India that can be accessed here in the states.

U.S. India Business Council

The U.S. India Business Council is a policy-level business advocacy group that represents the largest U.S. companies in India. Unless you're a heavy hitter or have a solid referral from a top executive in a *Fortune* 100 company, this group isn't where you'll want to invest too much of your time.

Focused Consultants and Intermediaries

For all intents and purposes, much of the initial business done in India is by reputation. Expecting to step off an airplane, pick up the telephone book, and let your fingers do the walking is a surefire recipe for disaster. You will need help if you expect to get things done when setting up a business there. Most international consultants have operations in

India staffed with credentialed professionals, but to really get things done you will want local help that is committed to your success and not just their fee.

Over the last thirty years, some of India's best and brightest have earned advanced university degrees in the United States and Great Britain. For personal, political, ethical, or family reasons, a good many returned home to follow their destiny and seek their fortune. Today, after years of hard work, they are successful leaders in Indian business, *Fortune* 100 companies, and within the Indian community. They are committed to helping all Indians realize their own potential as well as seeing India gain a leadership role in world affairs.

Many of these leaders have formed highly focused consultant groups with the goal of empowering all Indians to find leadership roles in the new economy. Along the way, they have developed and nurtured an extensive network of relationships throughout the top levels of Indian industry and commerce, upon which they now draw to further this work. I am fortunate to have had a personal, long, and prosperous relationship with the founder of one of these groups, one that is quickly becoming a leader in promoting this entrepreneurial vision and encouraging self-growth among India's young professionals. After speaking with appropriate government agencies to get "the view from 30,000 feet," your next step should be to meet with one of these focused consultancy groups.

You also should consider cultivating relationships with local trading firms, branch offices of major foreign banks and foreign law firms, and government commercial-agency bureaucrats. These people have their fingers squarely planted on the pulse of the local and regional business community. Not only can they be a wealth of information, they can also provide introductions to the intermediaries you need to meet.

Qualifying Partners, Agents, and Distributors

Odds are that you will be successful by using one or more of the options discussed above. However, there is the possibility that your newfound partner may not pass muster. Business-wise, India is a fairly informal country, and it's not unusual to have someone misrepresent his or her credentials, or worse. I know of one Indian fellow who successfully started two businesses and was working on a third, only to find that his partner was a crook who had stolen the rights for much of the assets. Is something like this inevitable or avoidable?

Issues of personal integrity, fraud, counterfeiting, and worse must be considered when performing due diligence on a potential Indian joint-venture partner or business acquisition. Quite frankly, the local police should be the last place to go for information or a recommendation. Instead, I strongly recommend retaining the services of a reputable firm that specializes in qualifying overseas partners and agents, such as Kroll, Inc., which has an office in New Delhi.

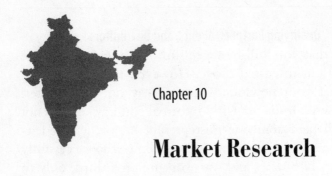

Chapter 10

Market Research

To be successful in India, more than any other country in the world, the savvy investor needs to have a clear and current picture of dynamic business conditions. Making timely decisions while trying to see around the next corner, so to speak, is crucial if the venture is to bring its backers the best yields and mandatory to avoid losing the business. Mastering these skills can be difficult, even for veteran investors, and requires a thoroughly comprehensive understanding of market factors and forces. The sooner these can be acquired, the better.

Regardless of the means one uses to gather data, the goal should be to collect and analyze as much quality information as possible with the time and budget available. One of the first decisions to make is how to conduct market research for the planned venture. Can it be assigned to staff in the home office, or should it be farmed out to professional consultants or market research services?

The urgent need for market research information has prompted several world-class firms to establish a presence in India. These firms complement the homegrown firms. However, there are a few drawbacks with using market research firms in India. One is that they are relatively expensive. Another is that their consumer/customer data may not be much better than data you can generate yourself. Finally, they may not be able to find the answers to some of your key questions, such as the quality and usefulness of the infrastructure around or between the areas you're considering. This type of information cannot be gleaned from an opinion poll.

Where Should You Start?

Presuming you've decided to do much of the legwork yourself, let's start here in the United States. Leaving the comfort of home or the office is not yet required. A great deal of big-picture information can be gleaned from numerous published sources, free as well as fee-based. Basic facts about India, like political conditions and macroeconomic changes, are reasonably easy to obtain. Pertinent business information, such as taxes, licenses, corporate laws, and insurance may require a few well-placed telephone calls or paid subscriptions to bona fide data-retrieval services. If there's no rush, then this research can be assigned to the company's audit and legal staff or part-time help.

In India, you will find that information is likely to be all over the map. It will take longer to process than anticipated and, if it's your first venture, may pose more questions than it answers. No matter how hard you may try and how much data mining you do, there will be significant gaps to fill.

Much of the important on-the-ground information, such as availability and quality of distribution networks, advertising media, locating and qualifying agents and salespeople, retaining business and office support staff, setting up bank accounts, permits, and local licenses, and uncovering hidden barriers to foreign business cannot be gathered from the United States. Still, other information is important enough that U.S. executives or business owners should want to stay directly involved, such as establishing personal security, safety, and relationships with potential Indian business partners.

Exporting to India, especially if the goods are destined for an SEZ or technology park near the port of entry, should be fairly painless. The Indian customer is doing all the hard work, in-country. Suppose, however, that the goals are to establish an Indian manufacturing presence and sell proprietary goods throughout the country and to export from India to one of its regional trading partners, or even back to the United States. Obviously, this is a much different situation that will require significantly more, and better, market research data on plant locations and distribution centers, quality and availability of local labor and management personnel, access to appropriate truck and rail transportation, and accommodations for visitors and expatriate staff.

One option is to organize the data needs into logical groups, assign responsibility for collecting and vetting the information to members of the corporate staff, and meet monthly for the next year while they shuffle this work into their regular assignments. Hopefully, business is so good that juggling won't be necessary or employee burnout the only predictable result. The prudent business owner or executive knows his or her own operation and staff well enough to decide whether or not this is the best way to proceed.

Another option is to retain the services of a specialized consultant who can spend the necessary time to meet with government officials, bureaucrats, and bank officers; attend appropriate functions and trade shows; identify competitors and potential partners; generate lists of potential customers; and locate candidate sales representatives, business agents, logistics, and transportation services. Here are a few tips to help you get the most from a consultant's services:

- Meet and contract with the persons who will be doing the work.
- Make contractually sure your study won't be farmed out or performed by the summer interns.

- Be certain that the consultants understand your overall objectives for doing business in India, including short-term as well as long-term plans.
- Set and agree upon clear goals, milestones, and levels of detail to be delivered.
- Find out, up front, what the consultants can and cannot do and how the work will be done, especially if plans to use proprietary or unfamiliar business models or analytical tools are proposed.
- Tell the consultants as much about your operation as you're allowed or feel safe to.
- Provide the consultants with as much of the unanalyzed data you're already collected so that they don't spend your time and money reinventing the wheel.
- Do much of the U.S. research yourself and assign the interviews with the pre-identified Indian resources to the consultants.

Internal Factors and External Risks

Now that you're at least committed to exploring India for its business potential, what should you be looking for to help frame your decisions? Does your management have a good grip on your business's internal factors? How well is your business suited to the endeavor? What changes will be required to make it happen? What factors are beyond your control? Is India a logical place for you to be looking at, now or some time in the future?

In my experience, it's always best to start from the top and work down. The way you choose to define "the top" is up to you and will be based on the size, nature, and experience of your operations. Regardless of how much or how little you know about India, the first step is to very clearly define the goal and then to determine how much risk can be tolerated.

For example, U.S. companies that manufacture for export might explore that route first. Are current Indian import regulations, tariffs, and taxes amenable to this approach, or are some or all of these conditions expected to change in two or three years? As a direct import, can your product be competitive now, in the future, or ever? Does India have trading partners to where the product can be imported and warehoused before it is re-exported to India under more favorable terms? Can a joint venture or business arrangement with an Indian partner circumvent traditional or legislated roadblocks? Might changing or amending your business approach make a venture more attractive? It may turn out that setting up a manufacturing facility or finishing plant is the best way to proceed. Is this feasible for your operation? Perhaps relocating your U.S. facility to India looks very attractive. How will it be financed? Do some usually ready sources of funding become off-limits to an approach like this?

Companies that provide services, such as those in engineering, construction, banking, and telecommunications, have different questions that will need to be asked and answered. Does India allow a permanent in-country presence for what you do? How much of the work can you perform from the United States? Does India or its states or union territories offer financial incentives or tax credits to set up operations there? Although English is India's second language, can enough sufficiently qualified people be found and hired? Will they be able to effectively communicate with your U.S. and European customers, for whom English could also be a second language?

Clearly, there is a real need to perform adequate and thorough market research before committing too deeply to a significant investment in India. External risks are constantly changing over there and managing a startup venture, even with a solid and committed partner, will take much time and effort.

There are several key macroeconomic and socioeconomic external risk factors that warrant investigating, both up front and after the venture is up and running. The ones I consider most important and have written and lectured on are listed below in no particular order. I'm sure that you also will be able to add a few of your own to this list. These are factors that you, I, and even the U.S. government have virtually no control over. It goes to say that all business plans should give these factors careful consideration and as wide a berth as can be tolerated. It's your turn now to find out what these factors mean to your business:

- Political instability at the national level
- Government interference at all levels
- Corruption at the state and local levels
- Public crime
- Social strife fueled by socioeconomic inequality
- Functional illiteracy caused by language differences and inadequate education systems
- Inadequate infrastructures
- Inflation and deflation in the national and local economies
- Inefficient banking and other financial institutions

From here on out, I'll be posing questions for you to answer rather than answering them for you. People at different levels and from many different businesses will want answers, but they're different depending on the situation. Also, what I could say here right now may have changed by the time you read this book.

Macroeconomic and Political Risks

As we're all aware, India has made commitments to its people and the rest of the developed world that, if achieved, will make her one of the world's largest economies within a generation. Having said that, and unless you are unusually well connected, your vision for ventures in India also should be long term in nature. You may not get rich as quickly, but your business is very likely to be there and successfully operating when your grandchildren are ready to take it over.

In this era of sound bites, segues, and slick phrases, it's crucial that you identify and use reasonably impeccable sources of information in India. Such sources are fairly conservative, and it's in their best interests to only deal with the facts. Examples of these sources are the U.S. Embassy in New Delhi; the American Chamber of Commerce in India; multinational banks, consulting and accounting firms; and branches and divisions of other U.S. companies in ventures similar to or different from your own. Cultivating relationships and initiating discussions with their representatives will help to learn the basics and stay informed on important questions, such as the following:

- What are the local political pundits saying about the Central Government and local governments?
- Are there rumors or reasons for change in India's domestic economic, monetary, or fiscal policies?
- Who are the political candidates looming on the horizon?
- How sound are India's relations with the United States and its business allies?
- Which market sectors are getting the most/least support from the Central and local governments?
- What U.S. companies have had the most/least success in India?
- What are the real forces behind India's domestic economy?
- Is India pinning its future on exports, imports, or domestic growth?
- How comprehensive and accurate are India's vital statistics?
- Can India's demographics help, hinder, or even halt its growth, and by how much?

- How deeply are the Central and local governments invested in industries?
- What are the government's plans to transfer these industries to private ownership?
- What are the trade barriers and incentives and domestic policies that discourage or attract foreign investors?

These questions also must be asked about governments at the state/territory and even local/municipal levels, especially in the major metropolitan areas, as the real economic power in India doesn't always lie in New Delhi.

The Fit for Your Business

The types of business ventures that foreigners are currently allowed to persue range from "all in" to "keep hands mostly off." Even for the all-in ventures, many of the realistic opportunities come with demographic limitations and geographic constraints that reduce near-term feasibility. Exporting allowable goods to India can be ponderous and fraught with tax and tariff barriers that quickly erode or wipe out profits. Importing goods from India may be desirable over there, but can their goods and services compete with U.S. domestic products or those sourced from other countries with established manufacturing sectors?

Perhaps the best bet for success is somewhere in between, through a joint venture with an Indian partner. Chapter 9 presented the major types of ventures available to the U.S. investor as well as some of the most important business issues that come attached to each. At this point, the best sources for the most detailed and current information on your proposed venture should be the nearest Consulate General of India in New York City, Houston, Chicago, or San Francisco or the Embassy of India, in Washington, D.C., both of whom can supply much of the key overview information you'll need to structure sound decision-making criteria. Some of the key questions you should be trying to answer include these:

- What are the specific laws governing foreign business ownership?
- What types of ownership are still restricted or reserved?
- Are there additional local and state constraints on business?
- Are there implicit requirements for local partners above and beyond any requirements of the Central Government?
- Do any local business regulations contradict Central Government laws?
- Would local or state regulations or practices implicitly or explicitly cause your U.S. operation to violate U.S. laws or the terms of your project's financing?
- How will your intellectual property be managed and protected?

Audit, Tax, Legal, and Licensing

Your company's accounting and legal officers are probably ill prepared to directly answer these questions for you. They can, however, work closely with major Indian accounting and law firms or Indian branches of major U.S. accounting and law firms to develop a clear picture for you and your board to review. Also, most of these firms publish timely newsletters, special reports, and even confidential "for your eyes only" studies on the implications of tax and legal changes. Information that you'll want at your fingertips should include the following, at a minimum:

- What requirements and schedules does India have for financial reporting?
- Do these reports require the review and approval of an India-registered auditor?
- Are the records of a foreign (that is, U.S.) business subject to review and audit?

- What are the details and requirements of the Income Tax Treaty between India and the United States?
- What are the current and proposed tax rates, and to what income do they apply?
- What is the status of tax incentives for foreign direct investment?
- What corporate or individual income is excludable or includable for tax purposes?

India's legal system is based on English common law, with limited judicial review of legislative acts. Historically famous for its ultra-lethargic judicial system and shadow economies, India also has separate personal-law codes for Muslims, Christians, and Hindus. One can quickly see that the underlying legal system in India functions differently from the one we are familiar with here in the United States. For example, the law governing contracts dates back to September 1, 1872. Furthermore, the many sweeping reforms India has seen over the past twenty years have generated a flurry of new and sometimes quirky policies and laws that are readily unenforceable. Laws governing Internet sales taxes, intellectual property, permits and licenses, worker termination and compensation, environmental protection, and women's rights are fairly new or still in draft form. Clearly, one needs the insight of a well-trained Indian attorney to navigate these choppy waters in safety. Here are a few questions for your corporate attorneys to consider:

- Which U.S. law firms have correspondents in India?
- Will there be problems or difficulties working with correspondent law firms?
- What are the current and anticipated laws governing business transactions, importing, exporting, and working in India?
- Are the incorporation and contract laws as simple as they appear to be?

- How involved are India's litigation laws?
- Can U.S. businesses run afoul of U.S. laws by obeying Indian laws?
- Can U.S. businesses, their Indian subsidiaries, and officers be held liable for criminal acts committed by its Indian agents, distributors, or employees?
- Will the U.S. or the Indian attorney review legal business documents?
- How well are intellectual property laws enforced?
- Who handles arbitration?

One question that might cross your mind and that is best asked discreetly is, "Should the venture fail and multilateral or bilateral lenders come looking for their money, who can I turn to in Washington and New Delhi for guidance and assistance?"

Insurance

Venturing into India can be risky to your business, your employees, and yourself. Indians traditionally seek compensation in the courts, which you'll want to avoid at all cost. Fortunately, U.S. and other multilateral and bilateral development agencies can insure your in-country plant and capital investments, and it's prudent to take advantage of these plans. But, what happens if your freshly assembled shipment of biomedical instruments never shows up at the airport in Mumbai? Can you get coverage in India for loss of exports you've manufactured there? Will they pay if the plane crashes or the ship sinks? Can you find a U.S.-based marine insurer to cover exports from India? Who pays when your rental car is involved in an accident? What happens if you or an employee falls ill or is injured at the plant? Will your U.S. plan cover you overseas?

Most HMO plans do not provide coverage for out-of-country claims. One option is to see if you can add a rider to cover these circumstances. If this cannot be done, specialized health-care bureaus are available that may offer coverage at a top Mumbai or Bangalore hospital as well as your travel costs back home.

Worker compensation insurance is not transferable, so you'll need to investigate this within India. The same generally holds true for product liability insurance, although some U.S. carriers may cover claims from India directly or through an Indian subsidiary or partner.

Large U.S. insurers, such as AIG, are forming joint ventures with Indian partners to provide personal, business, and corporate insurance coverage to members of India's new middle class and their employers. Logically, underwriters like these should be able to provide you and your venture with many of the types of coverage typically found in the United States and Europe. If your U.S. carrier is part of a joint venture or subsidiary arrangement, it's a good idea to see if the U.S. partner can write the policy here. Then premiums and claims can be handled stateside, leaving all the hard follow-up work to the carrier and its Indian partner.

In-Country Market Research

By now, you should have gathered about as much information as you can from U.S.-based sources. If exporting directly to India or through an offshore trading company is your forte, then you already may have enough information to get started. Additional information on product competition and options for distribution, advertising, and transportation to India is crucial; one trip there should give you the answers you need to make a decision.

On the other hand, if manufacturing wireless routers in India for the domestic market is your dream, you still have a way to go. At this point, you should be ready to mull and answer questions like these:

- Where are you thinking about building this plant?
- What do you know about local labor conditions, education, and availability?

- Is English spoken in the area?
- Can unassembled parts or raw materials be sourced in or brought into India at reasonable cost?
- Does India subsidize manufacturing or delivery of any or the entire product?
- Does the plant's steam and electricity stay on all day, or are rolling blackouts routine?
- Is the Golden Quadrilateral highway system actually completed and accessible in your area?

Anyone contemplating selling in India will need to build a sales force. Foreign entries in the retail sector are severely constrained, although some, such as in Wal-mart and Woolworths, are finding ways around this by acting as distributors and wholesalers to Indian retailers like Reliance and Godraj. Issues that are important to consider are these:

- Does India prohibit foreign sales personnel, other than those employed by a representative or liaison office?
- What regulations govern contracts between companies, foreign or Indian, and sales agents?
- Are sales agents allowed to represent competitor's products as well as their own products?
- Which business arrangements allow distributors to function as retailers?
- Are countertrade arrangements allowed under certain circumstances?
- Can Indian trading companies handle imported goods?

Soft Business Issues

It's likely that you're reading this book because you feel that India has potential as a market for your products or services. Many Indians will agree with you, but many also are a bit intimidated by the whole thing. That's because they've been doing business their own way for decades and the last thing they want to see is a new kid on the block. Informal cartels exist everywhere, and the locals know all the go-to people to solve their problems or to provide for their needs. You won't find any of this information on the Internet or in the local telephone book. The only way to get answers to these questions is to go to India.

Competition

Sending your money halfway around the world to a developing country can be intimidating. How much of an opportunity is this going to be for your firm? Who are you competing against? On the one hand, a Western view of India's relaxation of investment rules means opportunity. On the other, to established Indians at all levels, it could be interpreted as an economic invasion. The long list of business sectors still requiring Indian partners begs the question, "Am I being invited in to make money, or to be plucked?" Obviously, the answer depends a lot on whom you're working with and who's working for you. Let's look at retail.

Retail is one of India's most highly protected sectors and gets an inordinate amount of government scrutiny at high levels. As 97 percent of India's retailers (estimates put the number at over 15 million) are very small mom-and-pop businesses, distributors of consumer products are likely to encounter much of the low-level bureaucratic inefficiency as well as the caste-based power-broker networks that exist in India. Developing a good feel for how this works will shed some light on the overall level of law enforcement in everyday society.

Wholesale distribution is not protected, and doing business in this sector more clearly represents actual sales conditions in the country. Interviews of competitor's agents and salespeople should shed some light on how your venture might be received and handled by the locals. Chapter 3 emphasized the importance that caste, family, and kin have in Indian society. Thus, one might conclude that cartels and family networks could play a large role in the success or failure of any venture, a conclusion that is basically true.

For example, one of the biggest players in India's recent emergence is the Tata Group, a family business founded at the height of the British Raj in the middle of the nineteenth century. Google "Tata," and you will find that the group has positions in a large assortment of business sectors. Tata has successfully cultivated relationships with Western business leaders and leveraged these to create many joint ventures in important business sectors. The message is clear: if you want to virtually guarantee success, partner with a Tata Group company or another similar legacy firm.

This message applies to all business sectors. Similar networks should be anticipated at all levels in all professions and government. Personal relationships need to be identified and tactfully, and legally, cultivated in order to help get your startup arrangements, such as licensing/permitting, customs, local financing and banking, living arrangements, and work visas up and running. This is not entirely bad and, if handled properly, should afford you an easier time in cutting through the red tape and getting things done. The best people to learn from are those who have gone before you. Multinationals with established manufacturing facilities, sales offices, and sales forces know all the ropes and could be a good source of critical information. Information technology and business process outsourcing pros may also be willing to share their experiences, although the labor crunch in their sector could mean they'd rather not see anyone else enter the arena. India's construction boom has touched many companies in the architectural and engineering fields. Find out from them what they're seeing.

Advertising and Promoting Sales

First off, you must decide between two basic options: do your advertising and promotion yourself, or pay someone in

India to do it for you. Each option has its own strengths and drawbacks.

My advice is this: Unless your brand is universally recognizable, let a local agency or firm handle advertising and promotion for you, especially if your product or service is new to India or this is your first venture there. For the uninitiated Westerner, there are just too many cultural differences to assimilate, and a startup venture cannot afford to experiment for long to find out what works. And don't forget that if targeting major metropolitan areas throughout the country is your goal, you may have to run your advertisements in four or five languages. It's probably best to leave the translating to the locals.

The Advertising Agencies Association of India has Indian subsidiaries and joint ventures with most of the world's top agencies as well as many highly competent homegrown agencies. If these are too rich for your blood, the Association can steer you toward firms that fit your budget. A good advertising agency should be able to provide you with focused demographic information as well as recommendations for positioning your products or services. For example, they may advise you to change flavors or colors of food products to more closely mimic local culinary preferences. Traditional Hindus living outside major metropolitan areas are unlikely to buy beef products, so you may be advised to develop a vegetable-based substitute or even offer alternative products.

Delivering the message is equally important. India offers all the advertising media that we're familiar with here in the United States, plus a few that we're not. First and foremost are print media in the form of newspapers and magazines, as literacy rates are high in the major metropolitan areas. *The Times of India* and *India Today* are just some of the popular newspapers and newsmagazines read by middle- and upper-class Indians. Broadcast and cable television are probably the next most widely used media, especially in metropolitan areas, along with billboards and other poster/outdoor advertising. Direct mail is sparingly used. When it is, it's usually

business-to business promotion, which is good if you're selling management training courses but less so if toothpaste is
your principal product. Finally, the medium that's gaining
more attention in India than in the United States is showing
commercials at the local movie theater.

Government-Subsidized Activities

To attract investors, India has implemented across-the-
board tax breaks to some degree in almost every business
sector. For example, India has reduced or eliminated tariffs
on imports of raw materials and goods destined as inputs
to certain export-oriented manufacturing facilities. Income
taxes on export (from India) earnings have been exempted
from corporate income taxes.

Other areas where subsidies may be available to the foreign company, its Indian subsidiary, or joint-venture partner
include reimbursements for worker training, other exemptions from income taxes, and low-interest financing. These
may or may not be available in conjunction with loans or
grants from U.S. and multilateral or bilateral banks and
agencies. Some state governments offer subsidies and incentives for hiring and training local workers and for community involvement beyond the workplace.

Less obvious but still worth investigating are unannounced or unadvertised subsidies that are best uncovered
during a visit to a local or federal finance ministry office.
In cases like these, if your inquiry does not yield fruit, then
send in a local business contact or your Indian attorney.
They're more likely to uncover and obtain the terms and
requirements for these kinds of subsidies and should know
best how to present your plans to recalcitrant bureaucrats.
Also, depending on the nature and size of your project, you
can try proposing your own subsidies.

Labor, Shipping, and Transportation

Nearly every venture one can think of for India has
these three cost factors near to or at the top of their lists of

items needing control. Depending on where in the country you're looking, the uniqueness of each of these factors warrants careful consideration. Frankly, labor rates and worker benefits will be all over the map. Labor law requirements change depending on the number of employees you have at any one time. Unplanned changes in staff can trigger benefits or problems, depending on what changes you've made. Trying to hire qualified IT and BPO professionals is becoming more difficult and more expensive every day. Turnover rates are over 30 percent, and the average employee stays put for less than a year. Pay increases range from 10 percent to 20 percent, not including new-hire bonuses to the candidate and his referral.

Well, you get the picture. Are you planning to build apartment buildings with an unskilled labor component in your workforce? Just remember that many of these fellows migrate into the city from rural family-farming communities during the periods between crops. They'll be gone again when it's time to harvest or plant. Furthermore, the availability of skilled workers can be patchy. The local government office that administers laws on worker's rights and benefits is one place that you'll want to visit right away to find out about legally mandated fringe benefits, work hours, and minimum wages your company will be responsible for. Local craft-union halls also are good sources of information on wage rates, benefits, holidays, and other items related to the hiring and firing of skilled and unskilled workers.

Don't expect the unskilled (and even some skilled) workers to speak much, or any, English. You'll be relying very heavily on your managers and foremen to focus and motivate the rank and file. Finally, find out exactly how workers are hired, as human resource departments are a novelty in many Indian companies. You may be forced to retain a local recruiter or broker to find the skilled workers you need. Keep in mind that the average Indian is far more entrepreneurial than his American counterpart.

India's infrastructure is a Rube Goldberg contraption. Moving materials and products into, out of, and around the country is still difficult and there are many unknowns. Commuter rail service is probably the most reliable form of mass transportation in the country, yet its safety record is not good. Freight rail is a bit suspect. It may be fine in and around the mature areas of Maharashtra because that is the traditional heart of India's industrial base. In other areas it may not be as reliable.

There's been a big flurry of activity to repair, upgrade, and improve facilities in the most important ports. That's good if you're located near one of them. By all accounts, India's road system is poor. Many urban roads are too small, too decrepit, and far too overcrowded to be considered reliable enough for the purpose of scheduling shipments. Yet they may be all that's available for the next ten years. There are a few adequate long-haul expressways throughout the country; the Golden Quadrilateral system comes to mind. But one of the biggest complaints among shippers and truckers has to do with the tolls they encounter when crossing from one state or union territory into another.

If you're planning to manufacture for export or even some domestic distribution, consider one of the new Special Economic Zones or technology parks before committing to one of the older Export Oriented Units. These new free-trade zones and parks are far more modern, which translates into regular and ample electricity, steam, well-surfaced roads, better security, and easier access to railroads and airports. Establishing a presence in one of these zones triggers built-in tax breaks and other subsidies.

Can you source raw materials and capital equipment in-country? Can you get them to your facility in a timely manner, or at all? Can you deliver to customers in the same way? Will you need to import these items? Can they be imported? Carefully check and recheck all import requirements, especially licensing requirements. Contact local offices of U.S.-based trading companies, local trading companies, and in-country subsidiaries of U.S. companies in businesses like yours. Discuss their experiences with paying for shipments, delivery times, and how well or poorly shipments are handled. They can shed light on the informal requirements that you'll want to know about going in, such as finding out if the customs inspectors routinely solicit bribes before releasing shipped goods.

Foreign Exchange and Money Repatriation

The rules surrounding repatriation of money are still shrouded in mystery. Investors are frightened away by fears that their investments will be locked up forever. If that were the case, the biggest U.S. and European multinationals would not have established operations in India, and multilateral and bilateral development banks and agencies would not be guaranteeing loans and insuring foreign ventures. The Central Government continues to amend currency exchange control regulations in favor of foreign investors.

Current restrictions on currency transfers largely pertain to individuals and are grouped along the lines of foreigners, non-resident Indians, and resident Indians. The main issue centers on income taxes, and minor issues include residents moving their savings out of the country, which is frowned on by the domestic banking system, and money laundering. Also, foreigners and non-resident Indians are treated differently when it comes to investing in businesses. Many sectors are still partially protected, and these are the areas where repatriation fears are greatest. The best sources for current information are the Ministry of Finance, the Reserve Bank of India, or one of India's top banking institutions, such as the Bank of India, which has branches in major cities around the world. Also, the Indian Banks' Association acts as a repository for all current information on banking.

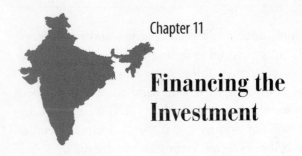

Chapter 11

Financing the Investment

According to the Indian prime minister's Economic Advisory Council, foreign direct investment inflows recently overtook foreign institutional investments into the country. According to the council, foreign direct investment in 2007 is expected to double that of the previous year—from $4.7 billion to $9 billion—while foreign institutional investment is expected to run at around $7 billion.

Establishing a presence in India can still be a risk that some investors want to spread. Aside from financing trade, which deals with moving goods and services into and out of the country (discussed in Chapter 12), financing direct investments requires a significant commitment on the part of the investor. As discussed in Chapter 8, direct investments mean the investor is literally putting both feet on the ground in India, regardless of whether it's a kiosk in a Mumbai shopping mall, a burger joint on the outskirts of Bangalore, or a million square feet of office and warehouse space in a Special Economic Zone near Kolkata.

All international business capital comes from these sources:

- World Bank
- International Monetary Fund
- Governments of wealthy nations
- Public debt
- Public equity
- Bank deposits

As a developing country, India relies heavily on international sources of financing. Its personal savings rates are good, at least among the one-third of the country's population that isn't living in poverty. The rapid growth of India's economy has generated much wealth for some of the people, and that wealth is looking for places to grow. Some of it finds its way out of the country, supporting the recent wave of overseas acquisitions. The rest stays home, largely in Indian banks, available for collateralized use.

There are several financial institutions and bodies that can finance direct investments in India:

- Overseas Private Investment Corporation
- U.S. Agency for International Development
- U.S. Trade and Development Agency
- United Nations
- Asian Development Bank
- Bilateral financial aid organizations
- Multilateral financial aid organizations
- Branch offices of foreign banks
- Local stock markets

Depending on the nature, size, and focus of the venture, one or more of these sources should be helpful to you. However, identifying specific programs and vehicles from within these institutions for your project or joint venture will be time-consuming and, at times, even frustrating. Don't be dissuaded. Each of these sources has programs for high-risk as well as low-risk ventures, with payment terms to match.

Most also have well trained and experienced staff members who will patiently guide you through the process and ensure that your valuable time is not wasted. After all, they're in the business of loaning money. Some are better than others at hand-holding, so be prepared to jump in and handle as much of the work as you can, if the need arises.

I believe that too many Americans underestimate the value of continually developing and nurturing relationships with financiers. Obviously, I'm not suggesting that you look for funds before you even have a legitimate venture. Rather, you ought to be networking with appropriate bankers and government agency representatives long before you find the ideal opportunity. These people are excellent resources for the kind of information you will need to develop a business plan, such as product pricing, business location, and even joint-venture partners. The good ones constantly have their ears to the tracks, so to speak, and can be good sounding boards for your ideas or help you focus your creative energy. Finally, even if they decide that your opportunity isn't for them, they should be more likely to steer you toward other viable financing options than to just wish you a good day.

The lending agency's perception of your venture will also affect how much effort they will commit. Having large projects in hot sectors and joint ventures with India's major players in hand will get you much better treatment than financing smaller, entrepreneurial ventures. This is where your persistence could spell the difference between failure and success. But recognize that some of these agencies just will not do business with you unless you have gold-plated credentials, are with a *Fortune* 100 firm, and are looking for access to many millions of dollars, or more. They've been entrusted by their own governments, other governments, and wealthy depositors to invest wisely, and so get to decide how much risk they're willing to take.

Overseas Private Investment Corporation

The Overseas Private Investment Corporation (OPIC) is an independent, U.S.-government–sponsored financial institution that provides medium-term and long-term loans and loan guarantees for foreign direct investment and project opportunities in underdeveloped and developing countries. OPIC can consider financing your venture, even after private-sector banks and insurers have turned you down, as long as it meets the following criteria:

- Is not listed in their categorically prohibited sector.
- Does not result in the closure of a U.S. operation or reduce your U.S. staff.
- Is not in a declining U.S. business sector (over the last ten years).
- Applies consistent and sound environmental standards.
- Upholds International Labor Organization worker-rights standards.
- Observes and respects human rights.
- Encourages positive development efforts in India.

Founded in 1971, OPIC historically funds projects, facilities, and franchises in the energy, natural-resource development, infrastructure, telecommunications, transportation, and housing sectors for U.S. corporations that are at least 50 percent owned by U.S. citizens and foreign corporations that are more than 95 percent U.S. owned.

Financing

For OPIC to consider a loan usually requires that the venture carries a debt-to-equity ratio in the 60/40 range and that the U.S. investor cover at least 25 percent of the venture, although having a brand-name franchisor, contractor, or operator on your team may mean you can get by with less. Interest rates are based on a combination of those in long-term capital markets and an assessment of the political and commercial risks associated with the venture. Businesses of virtually any size are conditionally eligible, and OPIC has several categories of loans based on the applicant's annual revenue:

- Under $35 million may qualify for Small Business Center financing.

- Between $35 million and $250 million may qualify for small and medium enterprise financing.
- Over $250 million may qualify for structured financing.

The Small Business Center is authorized to issue fixed-rate direct loans in amounts from $100,000 to $10 million, but for no more than 65 percent of the cost of the venture, with terms ranging from three to fifteen years. OPIC also offers direct loans with different parameters to medium-sized businesses. For financing larger projects and ventures, OPIC mostly offers loan guarantees up to $250 million per project and as much as $325 million for oil and gas projects. This latter maximum is down from $400 million, which was available as recently as 2005. Franchising ventures also qualify for OPIC funding, but the venture must demonstrate significant U.S. involvement and a long-term commitment on the part of the investor. Amounts from $100,000 to $1.5 million are available for single-unit investments, and amounts as high as $4 million are available for multiple-unit ventures. OPIC also offers partial guarantees on U.S. commercial bank loans, normally as high as 75 percent.

Political Risk Insurance

This is one of the real plums for the investor. OPIC offers political risk insurance for a wide range of investments and exports covering currency inconvertibility, expropriation, political violence (loss of assets and business income), and standalone terrorism (includes protection against chemical, biological, radiological, or other weapons of mass destruction). OPIC also offers special insurance products (coverage of institutional loans, capital markets transactions, and capital and operating leases) and products for certain business sectors (oil and gas, other natural resources, contractors and exporters, bid/performance/advance payments and other guarantees, project assets, customs bonds and disputes). U.S. small businesses, that is, those with annual revenues below

$35 million, can automatically insure their OPIC loans against losses from currency inconvertibility, expropriation, and political violence when they apply for their loans.

OPIC requires the investor to self-insure at least 10 percent of the venture, though third-party loans and capital leases from qualified financiers may be insured for up to 100 percent of the principal and interest. Premium base-rates for coverage range from 0.25 percent to 0.7 percent of the insured amount with a standby of 0.2 percent. Equity-coverage policies can extend for up to twenty years, while policies for ventures with limited durations can be had for the full term of the venture or project. For normal equity investments, OPIC provides coverage up to 90 percent of the original investment and 180 percent to cover future earnings. You should be aware that these percentages will change depending on how much exposure OPIC is willing to accept.

Although not available for ventures in India, the OPIC quick-cover insurance product is available for qualified ventures in several countries of strategic importance to India—Bangladesh, Pakistan, and Mauritius.

U.S. Agency for International Development

The U.S. Agency for International Development (USAID), an "independent government agency that provides economic, development and humanitarian assistance around the world in support of U.S. foreign policy goals," is administered by the U.S. Department of State and receives its guidance and direction from the secretary of state. Almost exclusively a government-to-government agency, USAID has as its goal the providing of assistance to economically disadvantaged foreign governments by stimulating economic growth, promoting higher living standards, and improving foreign exchange. USAID is headquartered in Washington, D.C., and, for over fifty years, has conducted its Indian operations from the U.S. Embassy in New Delhi, where it focuses on economic growth, health, disaster management, energy and the environment, and equity and opportunity for the citizens in India and the region as a whole. Although USAID has operated in India for two generations, its long-term goal is the phased reduction of support and to eventually eliminate its presence as India becomes self-sufficient. To achieve this goal, USAID is actively fostering partnerships with private entities, intermediate service organizations, and nongovernmental organizations that will, in time, assume many of its roles.

USAID operates special private offices that arrange funding for programs that improve worker and managerial skills and capabilities, identify ways to overcome technical obstacles to exporting and marketing, and locate capital and credit for financial intermediaries. Each year, USAID awards around $4 billion in foreign-assistance-program–oriented federal contracts and grants for technical assistance, equipment, and commodities in support of relief efforts or contracts, transportation services, and construction.

U.S. Trade and Development Agency

The U.S. Trade and Development Agency (TDA) mission is to "advance economic development and U.S. commercial interests in developing and middle-income countries . . . by funding various forms of technical assistance, investment analysis, training, orientation visits and business workshops." TDA gives special emphasis to economic sectors and ventures that may benefit from consulting and export of U.S. goods and services. The MENASA (Middle East, North Africa, South Asia) Regional Team located in Bangkok, Thailand, administers TDA activities in India.

United Nations Agencies

The United Nations administers two of the largest financial institutions in the world, the World Bank and the International Monetary Fund. In reality, the World Bank is really five development institutions, called the World Bank Group.

The first two are the International Bank for Reconstruction and Development (IBRD), which focuses on middle-income and creditworthy poor countries, and the International Development Association (IDA), which focuses on the world's poorest countries. Their mission is to "facilitate foreign direct investment into developing countries to support economic growth, reduce poverty and improve peoples lives" by doing the following:

- Insuring investors against political and noncommercial risk.
- Mediating disputes between governments and investors.
- Advising governments on how to attract investments.
- Serving as a repository for shared investment information.

In terms of World Bank funding, India qualifies for assistance as a "blend" country. It is sufficiently creditworthy to obtain IBRD loans and also qualifies for IDA financing due to its low per-capita income. India is in the top five of IDA borrowers worldwide. (Pakistan is first, and Bangladesh is sixth.) For the fiscal years from 2005 through 2008, IDA and IBRD have funded or have under consideration projects and programs in India totaling $5.9 billion and $9.6 billion, respectively.

The World Bank Group also has three private-sector development resources: the International Finance Corporation (IFC), the Multilateral Investment Guarantee Agency, and the International Center for Settlement of Investment Disputes. Together, these agencies function as multilateral lenders to member (foreign) governments and to private-sector ventures in developing countries.

International Finance Corporation (IFC)

IFC invests in emerging market companies and financial institutions. Its main activities are for-profit financing (equity, intermediate, trade, and quasi-equity) and risk management products, although its role has begun to broaden into technical assistance, anti-corruption, and social and environmental guidance.

Unlike borrowing from OPIC or USAID, investors in Indian ventures and projects can contact IFC directly with a proposal. IFC expects the owners to take the majority of the risk associated with a project or venture. For new ventures, IFC will usually capitalize up to 25 percent and, in special cases, as high as 35 percent. It will go higher for expansion projects, but at these levels it becomes increasingly wary of risk.

In India, IFC has provided well over $4 billion in financing to companies since 1956. India is currently the third-largest country in which the IFC is conducting operations, and its active role in U.N. sustainable development initiatives means it will be there for some time to come.

Multilateral Investment Guarantee Agency

The Multilateral Investment Guarantee Agency (MIGA) provides investment guarantees, technical assistance, and dispute-mediation services, all of which are designed to give investors and insurers confidence in making investments and doing business in traditionally difficult countries and regions. Equity investments up to $200 million can be insured up to 90 percent, and debt up to 95 percent. Larger ventures are insurable, but borrowers will need to seek syndicated coverage from MIGA. Coverage can be obtained for periods up to fifteen years—and beyond, under special circumstances—and can be reduced or terminated by the insured any time after the third year. MIGA can only terminate coverage if the guarantor defaults.

MIGA's forte is helping move financial decisions off the fence, where their progress has been stalled by uncertain host-country government actions, project complexity, and inadequate investment protection, and into play where they can do the most good by creating jobs and tax income, developing a skilled workforce, and stabilizing political, social, and environmental conditions. MIGA points to the following as areas in which its presence makes a real difference:

- Infrastructure development
- High-risk countries and markets
- Low-income countries and markets
- Conflict-affected areas
- South-South investments

MIGA is best known for managing political risk through the following guarantees and insurances, which may be combined in any way to suit the venture:

- **Currency transfer restrictions:** Provides protection against an investor's losses due to unforeseen foreign-exchange restrictions on converting profits, capital, interest, royalties, and loan principal from rupees back to U.S. dollars, euros, or another U.N.-member-country currency. Coverage also insures against unreasonable delays in obtaining exchange due to host-country inaction or omissions. It does not provide protection against currency devaluations on either side.
- **Expropriation:** Provides protection against losses due to hostile and aggressive business practices by host-country governments that may reduce or terminate the owner's rights to the insured investment; partial losses; and creeping losses, which are recognizable as a series of acts over a long period of time that eventually result in asset expropriation. It does not provide protection for losses due to host-country actions taken in accordance with its legitimate regulations and laws.
- **War and civil disturbances:** Provides protection against losses from damage or destruction of business property and assets from politically motivated acts of war, civil disturbances, revolutions, insurrections,

terrorism, sabotage, and even forcible changes in government (such as a coup d'etat).

- **Breach of contract:** Provides protection against losses from a host-country government's breach or repudiation of a contract agreement after arbitration or invocation of another valid dispute resolution mechanism was unsuccessful.

MIGA bases prices for its premiums on risks for doing business in the host country. Risks for investment in India, as evidenced by IBRD/IDA practices, are fairly low for a developing country. Rates range from 0.45 percent to 1.75 percent basis points per year.

MIGA also offers coverage for smaller ventures through its Small Investment Program, which insures against losses due to currency inconvertibility and transfer restrictions, expropriation, and war and civil strife. It does not insure against losses due to breach of contract or projects expected to produce significant adverse impacts to existing environmental conditions. The program is not restricted to small and medium-sized investors, although its clear intent is to facilitate the involvement of these investors in development projects by waiving their application fee. MIGA defines a small and medium investor/enterprise as the following:

- Having no more than 375 employees
- Have no more than $50 million in assets
- Have no more than $100 million in annual sales

This coverage also is available to ventures in the financial sector provided the venture is geared toward financing small and medium enterprises and at least half of its clients are small and medium enterprises, as defined below. To qualify for coverage under the Small Investment Program, the venture or project must invest in a venture with the following:

- A maximum of 300 employees
- Total assets of $15 million, or less
- Total annual sales of $15 million, or less

Under the Small Investment Program, clients are required to assign all securities, stocks, and assets over to MIGA unencumbered.

Development Banks

There are four regional development banks around the world that, together with the World Bank Group, are collectively referred to as multilateral development banks. These four independent regional banks fund private projects and businesses, government infrastructure projects, and endeavors that are part of environmental and health-related programs. They also can provide guidance to other smaller or more specialized lenders when the project or venture doesn't fit their mold, so to speak. In addition to the regional development banks, smaller development banks, which are privately funded or owned by governments, regional trade organizations, industry consortia, local businesses, and local banks and commercial banks, often finance ventures in-country and in regions.

Asian Development Bank

The Asian Development Bank, which is headquartered in Metro Manila, Philippines, serves India from its India Resident Mission in New Delhi. The Asian Development Bank includes members from many countries within and outside the region, as well as donor and borrowing countries. Its stated mission is the reduction of poverty and improvement of the quality of life of all citizens in its developing-country members by emphasizing a private-sector development strategy. Together, these form the bank's long-term strategic framework. The Asian Development Bank accomplishes this through the following means:

- Loans
- Grants
- Technical assistance
- Guarantees
- Equity investments

As you can see, at the global level governments are heavily invested in providing or guaranteeing viable sources of capital for almost any type of venture. And, yes, there are more options if the World Bank or MIGA aren't right for your particular venture.

Multilateral Financial Institutions

In addition to the development banks, several other banks and funds lend to developing countries. These multilateral financial institutions function independently and, because of their focus and size, tend to have a narrower or specialized focus on the business sectors and activities they invest in.

International Fund for Agricultural Development

The International Fund for Agricultural Development (IFAD) is a specialized agency of the United Nations and functions at the government-to-government level. IFAD provides loans to U.N. developing-member countries for approved projects and programs, and serves India from its country program management office in Rome, Italy. Terms and conditions vary according to the borrower's per-capita income. IFAD also provides grants to institutions and organizations to support activities that strengthen the technical and institutional capacities essential and corollary to agricultural and rural development. Grants are limited to 10 percent of the combined loan and grant program.

IFAD rural development projects focus on assisting the rural poor and indigenous populations to increase food production, raise personal incomes, and improve public health, nutrition, and education standards.

IFAD supports ventures and projects in agricultural development, micro- and macro-financial services, rural infrastructure, livestock, fisheries, capacity and institution building, food processing and storage, marketing, research, extension, training, and small and medium enterprise development.

Nordic Investment Bank

Headquartered in Helsinki, Finland, the Nordic Investment Bank (NIB) is the common international finance institution for the five Nordic countries and Estonia, Latvia, and Lithuania.

NIB finances all types of project costs, including local costs, for private and public projects within the Nordic countries as well as in other areas of the world, and has financed work in India. NIB remains flexible in terms of supporting different areas of the economy but puts particular emphasis on projects involving infrastructure, environmental improvement, large corporate investments, and small and medium enterprises in cooperation with financial intermediaries. The projects should be of mutual interest to India and the bank's member countries. Loans are usually granted on a sovereign basis but may also be granted without a government guarantee, such as to private-sector infrastructure investments. In India, NIB was most recently involved in financing port development projects.

For projects larger than 25 million euros, investors should contact the European Investment Bank, of which NIB is a member.

European Investment Bank

The European Investment Bank (EIB), headquartered in Luxembourg, can provide long-term loans to public and private-sector borrowers for up to 50 percent of existing productive ventures and projects in India, usually with requirements of an Indian-government guarantee. These come in the form of individual loans for capital spending programs or projects greater than 25 million euros and global loans to banks and financial institutions to finance customers with smaller eligible spending programs or projects costing less than 25 million euros. Terms of the loans vary from ten to twelve years for industrial projects and up to fifteen to twenty years for infrastructure projects. In India and throughout much of the developing countries of southern Asia, EIB focuses largely on loans for use in development, aid, and cooperation projects applied to infrastructure upgrades, energy, telecommunications, reduction of environmental impacts, education, and manufacturing. EIB does not provide venture capital, which should be solicited from the European Investment Fund.

OPEC Fund for International Development

The OPEC Fund for International Development (OFID) is an intergovernmental development finance institution established and funded by the members of the Organization of the Petroleum Exporting Countries (OPEC). Its purpose is to promote cooperation between OPEC member counties and other developing countries, particularly poorer and low-income countries, in an expression of South-South camaraderie. From its lavish headquarters in Vienna, Austria, OFID administers financing, loans, and grants for the following:

- Development projects and programs, and support for balance of payments
- Technical assistance, food aid, and research
- Supplemental support of other development institutions in developing countries
- Private-sector activities in developing countries

Through 2006, OFID has committed over $222 million in public-sector loans to projects and programs in the agriculture and agro-industry, education, energy, health, general industry, development banks, transportation, water supply, and sewerage sectors.

Bilateral and Country Development Agencies

India has been phasing out its bilateral relationships with smaller-country development agencies. In some instances, such as Australia, the Indian government is now receiving government aid through Australia's contributions to the United Nations and to multilateral development banks. Also, other small, politically neutral countries like Sweden terminated their own development-banking relationships with India after its 1998 nuclear-weapon tests were announced. This has created something of a moving target for those investors looking to these types of bilateral development banks and agencies for assistance. However, patience and thorough research should turn up viable sources for most ventures and projects as these banks and agencies are often amenable to orienting investors toward viable alternatives. Here is a sampling of development agencies active in India.

German Investment and Development Company

The Deutsche Investitions–Und Entwicklungsgesellschaft mbH (DEG), headquartered in Cologne, Germany, provides long-term capital for private-sector ventures in developing countries, only taking on commitments in projects that make a beneficial development policy impact, meet environmental standards, and comply with social principals. DEG focuses on private-sector projects in agribusiness, infrastructure, and renewable energy, and is interested in projects in mining, manufacturing, tourism, capital market activities, biotechnology, communications, IT, and pharmaceuticals. Although DEG is most comfortable when assisting German companies, it does not preclude India-centric investors from other countries. DEG can provide the following:

- Long-term loans up to 25 million, in either euros or U.S. dollars, with terms between four and ten years and often secured with fixed assets in India.

- Equity capital participation in the project from 5 percent to 25 percent, with clearly defined exit strategies and the possible requirements for seats on the board of directors.
- Mezzanine financing with risk-oriented yields, subordinated security, and conversion rights.
- Guarantees for long-term loans or bonds in rupees, with a reduced exchange-rate risk through loan repayment in rupees and risk sharing with Indian banks.

Germany takes great pride in being one of India's five most important investment partners. Currently, over 1,500 German companies have direct investments of one sort or another in India.

Industrialization Fund for Developing Countries
The Industrialization Fund for Developing Countries is a wholly owned agency of the government of Denmark. It provides loans, guarantees, and equity capital for commercially viable joint venture projects in developing countries that promise a return of capital within eight to ten years. The fund also finances feasibility studies and technology transfers and offers training grants. Like other European agencies, the Industrialization Fund for Developing Countries prefers to work with Danish private-sector partners and takes a minority position, usually no greater than 30 percent, in all its investments. It looks for projects that conform to the developing countries' growth goals, and will reject, outright, proposals for ventures that will adversely impact human health and the environment.

Indian Banks and Branches of Foreign Banks in India
It wouldn't be prudent to overlook Indian development banks, commercial banks, and branches of U.S. commercial banks as possible sources of financing for the in-country part of a joint

venture. Examples include the Industrial Development Bank of India, ICICI Bank, and HDFC Bank. Standard Charter Bank, which is based in India, is partly owned by foreign banks as a result of a merger in the 1990s. Consolidation in the Indian banking sector is a hot topic of discussion right now. Like everything else in India, however, this may have changed by the time you read this book.

The Reserve Bank of India continues to open the door a little at a time for foreign banks that want to set up operations in India, and everyone is cautiously confident that this is only the beginning of a new era in foreign banking in India. Foreign banks in India are permitted to set up local subsidiaries, but they may not acquire Indian ones (except for weak banks identified by the Reserve Bank of India, on its terms) and their Indian subsidiaries will not be able to open branches without government approval. Countries with banks in India include the Netherlands, United Arab Emirates, Ceylon, France, the United States, the United Kingdom, China, Germany, Canada, Bahrain, Scotland, and Switzerland. A partial list includes the following:

- ABN AMRO
- Abu Dhabi Commercial Bank
- Bank of Ceylon
- BNP Paribas
- Citibank
- China Trust Company
- Credit Suisse
- Deutsche Bank
- GE Capital
- HSBC
- Industrial and Commercial Bank of China
- J.P. Morgan Chase
- Royal Bank of Scotland
- Standard Charter Bank

- Scotia Bank
- Taib Bank
- UBS

Supplier Financing

Here in the United States, it's not uncommon for small businesses to look to their suppliers for extensive credit or even upfront financing of a new venture. I can't understand why some suppliers would consider it, but they do. So, if you're looking to enter India with a unique product or service that can pass through import regulations with little or no tariffs or duty fees, you might want to consider structuring a deal with your supplier. He will help finance the venture by covering your costs for his products until you can start making sales and turning a profit. You do give up some control and might have to give your supplier personal guarantees, because once the goods are in India they're not coming back. However, this will enable you to take advantage of an opportunity far more quickly than you otherwise could by pursuing financing through the SBA or other multilateral provider. In more complicated cases, you might consider using countertrade (discussed in Chapter 13) as one component of the financing package.

Investment Banks and Private-Equity Financing

Right now, private-equity financing by investment banks is the hottest topic in India. Investment banks raise capital by selling securities, acting as intermediaries for clients wishing to trade securities, underwriting bond issues, and advising clients. Investment banks traditionally are not a viable source of capital for financing business acquisitions by a third party, such as you or me. What they hope to be able to do in the future is help you prepare the initial public offering for the Indian company you purchased with help and financing from USAID, the SBA, or a commercial bank in India.

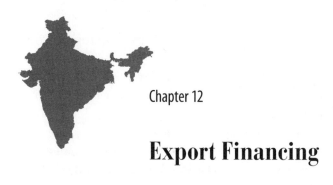

Chapter 12

Export Financing

In an ironic twist, India's post-Independence closed-door policies paved the way for the U.S. exporter to finance shipments and sales into the subcontinent. In an attempt to protect Indian banks, the Foreign Trade (Development and Regulation) Act of 1992 created an interesting condition/situation. One of India's requirements for a foreign bank to set up an operation/joint venture in India was that its home country had to give reciprocity to an Indian bank. The result of this tit-for-tat policy is that many top Indian commercial banks have offices in America's major cities. The correspondent relationships that have been established between these banks and their U.S. counterparts virtually guarantee at least one financing option for your exports. Your company's own hard-earned capital can then be used for more productive endeavors.

Determining Creditworthiness

No evaluation of financing options can be done until the creditworthiness of the importer/buyer and exporter/seller is gauged by using standard sources, references, techniques, and methods. Many private, commercial, bilateral, and multilateral lenders and guarantors will not move on an application without this information. Of course, venture capital is also a viable source in the absence of good hard data, but unless the payback terms are right, it's probably not the best way to go. The exporter/seller simply gives up too much in the deal.

The recent opening up of the Indian economy has been so explosive that credit reports should be carefully scrutinized. Doing business with the Indian subsidiary of a well-known multinational may not be too risky, but selling millions of dollars of capital equipment to a Small-Scale Industry startup in a Special Economic Zone could be problematic. The U.S. Department of Commerce can provide reports on the creditworthiness of some companies. Also, private business data providers, like Dun & Bradstreet, and export factors can help.

This is one area where uncertainty will be the norm for several years to come. On the other hand, the Indian economy is growing so rapidly that nearly every venture is a winner, and selling to well-managed, well-financed buyers may be worth enough to take the chance. You will have to be the judge.

Commercial Banks

Commercial banks are the lifeblood of international trade. Businesses and countries could not import, export, invest, conduct countertrade, make wire transfers, conduct currency arbitrage, issue and pay documentary letters of credit, or handle foreign exchange conversions without them. Even though they do not have to be the actual source of the capital, the safest legal way to conduct business overseas is for all money transfers, payments, and collections to go through them. All of the export finance, credit, and loan guarantees discussed in Chapter 11 use commercial banks to handle the transactions between lending agencies, government central banks, and the foreign customer or U.S. exporter.

Are all banks equal? No. You should spend some time working with the bank you use for your business to discuss and identify a good commercial bank that has the experience and credentials to handle your export financing. This could be a U.S. commercial bank, a U.S. full-service bank that has an international department, or even the U.S. office of an Indian commercial bank, depending on your particular needs. Once several candidates have been identified, an exporter should determine and confirm the following about each:

- Its international department has a great deal of experience with a wide variety of options and instruments.
- It can handle foreign currency transactions without having to go through another commercial bank or other money-center bank.
- It has very good relationships with reputable correspondent banks in India and elsewhere (for example, Mauritius).
- It does not require additional collateral for exports being partly funded by U.S.-government–supported guarantees.
- Its loan officers and executives are very familiar with all forms of letters of credit.

You should not consider using a bank that cannot provide complete and comprehensive information on all of these criteria. The prudent exporter should also retain the services of a consultant or professional who is highly experienced with documentary letters of credit. These individuals are often retired officers of commercial banks.

There are two principal sources of export credit: those supported by the U.S. government, and those extended by private lenders or creditors. U.S.-government–supported financial aid programs tend to be selective of the goods, services, markets, and types of firms they will deal with. For example, the U.S. Export-Import Bank (Ex-Im Bank) was involved in the ill-fated Dabhol Power Project orchestrated by Enron with the Indian state of Maharashtra. When the project fell apart, Ex-Im Bank was able to muster the full weight of the U.S. administration to bear on the affected parties. However, Ex-Im Bank won't do this for everyone, as you might have surmised. Still, there are a multitude of other federal and state government programs, private associations and organizations, international banks, and insurance programs that may work for you.

Private-Sector Organizations

Without exaggerating, it's safe to say that there are hundreds, if not thousands, of private-sector finance sources. Some examples are spin-offs from defunct government-supported trade-advisory boards; privately owned manufacturing, shipping, trading, or distributing organizations and companies; subsidiaries of investment and commercial banks and credit unions; and even manufacturers themselves. The benefit of obtaining financing from one of these groups is that they are less likely to use the export business's solvency or credit rating as the loan qualifier. Instead, they're more interested in the viability of the transaction and will use this as a significant determinant in approving or denying the financing.

Payment Terms

There are several popular payment terms that can be used, all of which use the exporter's own credit or assets as security. Each has its own merits and shortcomings and should be used with caution. Here are a few examples:

- **Open account, or sales on consignment:** This is nothing more than a promise to pay, the simplest to effect but far too risky to recommend. Salespeople love open account, but the company's financial department does not.
- **Cash:** This is useful if one wants to avoid certain minor taxes.
- **Clean drafts:** Similar to open account, here the draft goes to the importer's bank for collection.

- **Time draft:** The importer promises to pay at the specified time upon acceptance of the draft.
- **Sight draft:** The importer pays the draft "on sight."

You should be able to use one or a combination of these payment terms for most of your business transactions.

Payment Schedules

The other key factor in choosing financing is time. Export financing is usually classified as short term (payment made in under 180 days), intermediate term (payment periods up to five years), and long term (payment periods longer than five years). Since the mid-1990s, India has made several changes to its foreign currency exchange laws that have a direct bearing on financing exports into the country. Here are some of the recent restrictions, as pointed out by the U.S. Commercial Service:

- Indian importers can freely make limited down payments, in U.S. dollars, outside the country for certain capital products (such as machinery).
- Above a certain dollar amount, the importer must obtain a bank guarantee for the full amount, and the full shipment should be received within ninety days.
- Short-term credit cannot exceed 180 days.
- A deferred import license may be required when deferred-payment credits on capital goods and similar shipments extend beyond thirty days—usually up to six months and beyond.

Again, changes occur frequently, so always check with the Reserve Bank of India, a U.S. branch of a major Indian commercial bank, or a major U.S. commercial bank for current information.

Short-Term Financing

As noted above, short-term financing applies to payment terms of no more than 180 days. The most talked-about method is the open draft or sale on consignment. However, like other exporter-financed arrangements, it should not be used unless the business relationship between the exporter and the importer is ironclad, the deal is fully secured with accessible collateral, and the importer's credit is beyond reproach. Otherwise, it is simply too risky. The most popular forms of short-term financing are the Documentary Letter of Credit and the Documentary Banker's Acceptance.

Documentary Letter of Credit

The documentary letter of credit is actually a sophisticated, orchestrated process through which the exporter, importer, commercial banks in both countries, and the shipper all have specific documentation responsibilities and roles to play. When properly done, the letter of credit is reasonably foolproof. However, it is never a guarantee of payment.

A reasonably sound letter of credit can contain well over twenty separate pieces of information. Also, the exporter affords himself far more protection by ensuring the letter of credit is irrevocable and confirmed on a commercial bank in the United States (that is, the exporter's country). Obviously, if the exports are originating elsewhere, then the banking arrangements may change. Some of the major items identified in the letter of credit are the following:

- Opening bank (the importer's commercial bank)
- Advising or confirming bank (the exporter's commercial bank)
- Terms of sale
- Revocability or irrevocability
- Documentation requirements
- Amount of credit
- Payment terms

- Opening and closing dates of the letter of credit
- Shipment terms
- Letter-of-credit transmittal terms

Dotting the i's and crossing the t's are a must when using letters of credit to finance exports because there are many clever ways that unscrupulous importers (and their banks) can void a letter of credit. Here are just a few:

- Misspelling of names and addresses
- Inaccurate or incomplete descriptions of payment terms, prices, and merchandise
- Nonconforming or incomplete documentation
- Incorrect dates on documentation that are outside the terms of the letter of credit
- Delivery of documentation beyond the expiration date of the letter of credit
- Mismatches between language in the bills of lading and invoices and the letter of credit

Variations of the Documentary Letter of Credit

Export and import transactions come in many different varieties. The presence of third parties in the deal, distribution of risk, and complex shipping arrangements can all affect how the letter of credit is negotiated and written. Here are just a few:

- **Assigned proceeds:** Assigns the proceeds from the letter of credit to the exporter's suppliers, essentially using the buyer's credit as collateral for working capital.
- **Back-to-back letter of credit:** This uses the letter of credit between the seller and the buyer as collateral for a second letter of credit (of longer duration) between the seller and its suppliers, which enables the seller to get paid before paying the suppliers.

- **Off-balance-sheet credit extension:** This also uses the letter of credit between the seller and the buyer to issue a second letter of credit, except this new letter of credit is issued directly to the supplier from the bank.
- **Standby letter of credit:** This is issued by banks as alternatives to bank guarantees, and are often used as contractor bid and performance bonds, guarantees against various forms of payment, and performance guarantees against advance payments.
- **Transferred letter of credit:** This is used when the goods are shipped directly from the supplier/manufacturer to the buyer, essentially reducing the exporter's role to that of an intermediary in the transaction by transferring the letter of credit directly from the buyer to the supplier.

Documentary Banker's Acceptance

Similar to factoring, the documentary banker's acceptance is used when the seller wishes to use its own credit as security for a sale. Once the goods are shipped, the documentation is sold to a bank at a discount. Often, foreign buyers that are having difficulty proving their creditworthiness will cover the fees to ensure the sale goes through and the shipment is made.

Clean Banker's Acceptance

In a clean banker's acceptance, a letter of credit is not used for collateral. Rather, the exporter's own credit serves that purpose. The exporter still sells the transaction to the bank at a discount, but the bank then sells the draft on the secondary bond market. Clean banker's acceptances typically run around $750,000, although they do go lower, and are frequently used by large multinationals whose credit is normally beyond reproach.

U.S. Bank Branches in India

Perhaps the simplest way to finance exports is to use Indian branches of U.S. banks. All that is necessary to do this is for the exporter's bank to have a branch in India or a line of credit with a bank in India. Depending on the type of transaction, the bank may want a guarantee from Ex-Im Bank or another guarantor agency.

U.S. Small Business Administration

The U.S. Small Business Administration (SBA) has developed several vehicles to help U.S. small businesses succeed in the international marketplace. These include training, education, and loans. The SBA offers three loan programs to assist with developing or expanding export markets.

SBA Export Express

To be eligible for Export Express, the business must be able to qualify for an SBA loan guarantee and have been in operation for at least one year, although it is not required to have been in exporting during that year. The loans may be used for the following purposes:

- Financing export development activities, such as participating in trade shows or having product literature translated into Hindi or another Indian language
- Financing transaction-specific overseas orders
- Revolving lines of credit for export purposes
- Buying or improving U.S. facilities and equipment to produce exports or services for exports
- Financing standby letters of credit for use as bid or performance bonds

The SBA guarantees loans on a sliding scale: 85 percent up to $150,000, and 75 percent over $150,000, up to a maximum of $250,000.

Export Working Capital Loans

This program offers a 90 percent guarantee up to $1 million for working capital to support single transactions or multiple (revolving) sales. In addition to interest, the loans mature in one year and require a 0.25 percent fee on the guaranteed portion. It may be used for the following purposes:

- Purchasing finished goods and acquiring inventory for export
- Financing pre-export costs of labor and materials used to manufacture exports
- Financing costs of U.S. labor and overhead for service-company exports
- Financing standby letters of credit for use as bid or performance bonds
- Financing foreign receivables

The loans may be secured with assets; assignment of proceeds from letters of credit, documentary collections, and foreign receivables; personal guarantees; and liens on the inventory.

International Trade Loans

SBA International Trade Loans are aimed at supporting the development of exports or assisting small businesses adversely affected by competition from imports. These loans cannot be used for refinancing debt. With this program, SBA can guarantee up to $1.25 million in combined working capital and equipment and facilities loans with maturities as long as twenty-five years, depending on the combination of loans requested by the exporter. The two main conditions are that fixed assets financed with the loan must be within the United States, and working capital financed with the loan must meet the requirements of a standalone SBA Export Working Capital Loan. A fee of 0.25 percent is charged for loans with maturities under one year (working capital loan component), although permanent working capital loans may extend for 10 years.

An International Trade Loan must be secured on collateral located within the United States, and the lender must take a first lien or mortgage on the fixed assets.

Credit Insurance

As in financing direct investment loans, it's advisable to research and obtain credit insurance when the bank or the exporter feels there are significant risks. Political instability, expropriation, currency fluctuations, and failure to pay are just a few of the risks that the exporter should consider.

India is a fairly stable country and shows no signs of immediately nationalizing private firms, so the likeliest risk one might encounter is the importer's failure to pay after the goods are accepted.

Intermediate-Term Financing

For exports of capital goods and shipments where payment periods run up to five years, it's best to look for better terms than those available for short-term financing. Non-bank private-sector organizations also finance intermediate-term loans and should be given serious consideration. Other options include government-supported sources, such as Ex-Im Bank and the SBA's Export Working Capital Program, which provides working capital loans to finance export transactions. Lines of credit obtained through the SBA usually mature in one year, and working capital loans' maturity match simple transaction cycles.

There are several additional sources for intermediate-term financing that should be considered: forfaiting, export factoring, leasing, and the Private Export Funding Corporation (discussed on page 241).

Forfaiting

Forfaiting has been used in trade finance for many years and has become quite popular during the past forty years, largely in Europe by Italian and German corporations exporting high-value, long-term transactions. In its most basic form, forfaiting is very much like factoring receivables with an accompanying bank guarantee from the customer. These transactions require an exporter, an importer, the importer's guarantor (such as an Indian commercial bank), and a forfaiter. The exporter sells ("forfeits") for cash a receivable (fixed-rate, long-term debt) to a third party (forfaiter), who then assumes all the risk for collecting the debt from the importer. Then, the forfaiter either holds the debt or resells it in a specialized trading market.

Exporters are attracted to forfaiting when they are unable or unwilling to provide short-term or medium-term credit to the buyer. It's also very attractive because it covers the entire cost of the sale and is cheaper than borrowing from a commercial bank. Here are some other instances when forfaiting should be considered:

- The importer is unable to obtain bank financing.
- The importer demands fixed-rate financing from the exporter.
- The exporter is unable to obtain export credit insurance for the transaction.

Furthermore, as forfaiting becomes more popular, exporters may find they have to offer it to beat the competition and win the sale.

Export orders below $500,000 usually won't attract a reputable forfaiting house to a deal, although smaller and sector-specialized firms may express interest in orders as low as $100,000.

International (Export) Factoring

Factoring domestic receivables first appeared in India in the early 1990s, largely because small-size companies were finding it very difficult to collect receivables from medium- and large-scale companies. This bottleneck quickly caused a cash flow crunch as debts piled up faster than sales increased. However, export factoring is not the same thing as factoring domestic receivables. Ideally, export factoring involves the purchase of receivables without recourse by a "factor" for immediate cash at typical discounts ranging from 75 percent to 90 percent of the face value. As with forfaiting, the export factor then assumes all responsibility for collecting payment from the importer. Besides getting paid, the other clear benefit to an exporter is there usually is no lower or upper limit on the dollar amount of the receivable, although some export factors tend to shy away from very small receivables.

Factors also can be retained to perform financial management services, including financing, credit management, buyer-credit investigations, and ledger accounting (book-keeping). Some export factors offer a full service, by which they routinely purchase an exporter's receivables after sales are completed. Although factoring companies remain highly specialized institutions, many major international banks have factoring subsidiaries.

There are several large U.S., Indian, and Chinese export factors, including Citibank and HSBC, operating in India where the annual growth rate for export factoring exceeds 50 percent, with a total five-year turnover of around $2 billion.

Originally, textiles and clothing were the most popular receivables factored, but manufacturers of industrial and farm equipment, office equipment, electronics, and processed food are becoming more popular. Export factoring is attractive to small and medium-sized companies undergoing rapid growth because it can be used to eliminate risk, ensures trade-related cash flow, and can generate additional working capital.

If you really trust your buyer to make all of his or her payments on time, then factoring with recourse might cost less because the export factor does not need to assume risk for the potential default of the buyer.

Leasing

If you're in the right business, leasing—even with purchase options—to firms in India is definitely worth considering. The lease can be structured and managed by the exporter, contracted to a recognized leasing company, or handled through a venture or established lessor in India. Leasing can be an effective intermediate-term as well as long-term financing option, especially if it's the only way the sale can be completed.

There are several additional considerations that are part of international leasing that go above and beyond those encountered with domestic leasing of capital equipment. Examples of some of these are the following:

- Need for credit insurance
- Secondary collateral guarantees from the supplier
- Customs and international contractual differences
- Differences between Indian and U.S. tax codes

Leasing may not be the best approach for the smaller U.S. company, as the complexities of establishing an Indian presence often overshadow the benefits. The use of a reputable Indian lessor as part of the team is a feasible alternative because they meet all the following criteria:

- Know the local rules
- Are structured to take advantage of the income tax regulations

- Can use domestic financing to purchase the assets
- Are more attuned to changes in the business climate
- Can directly check the lessee's credit
- Can manage Indian customs and sales tax requirements
- Can arrange and administer insurance and collect lease payments

Most international leasing transactions are handled by leasing divisions or subsidiaries of commercial banks, merchant banks, and multinational investment banks.

Long-Term Financing

Long-term financing for international trade is the realm of government and bilateral banks and agencies. The dollar amounts that are involved can go well into the hundreds of millions, or higher, and most banks and private financiers are reluctant to directly tie up a big percentage of their assets in one or two ventures. However, organized groups of private financiers may be amenable to pooling their resources, provided they can get rock-solid guarantees. Another option used by many large multinational corporations is countertrade (described in Chapter 13), which is popular with the Indian government.

Export-Import Bank of the United States

The Export-Import Bank of the United States (Ex-Im Bank) is the official export credit agency of the United States. By assuming credit and country risks that the private sector is unable or unwilling to accept, Ex-Im Bank makes it possible for many exporters to compete in the international arena. The bank fully supports exports to India; there are no time or dollar-amount limitations on Ex-Im Bank assistance.

In the past, Ex-Im Bank has been criticized for disproportionately serving large manufacturing companies exporting capital equipment for massive overseas projects, such as the Dabhol Power Project in Maharashtra. In response to this criticism, the bank has created several focused initiatives, one of which is specially geared toward small-businesses' exports. The other focused initiatives pertinent to India address the transportation security, environmental, and medical equipment sectors.

Ex-Im Bank offers medium- and long-term financing that goes well beyond what individual banks can offer. As pointed out by Ex-Im Bank, the services it provides are as follows:

- Direct loans
- Pre-export financing and working capital guarantees
- Loan guarantees and export credit insurance
- Finance lease guarantees

In all its transactions, the bank counts lenders, insurance brokers, city-state trade agencies, and U.S. trade agencies as its partners.

Direct Loans

Ex-Im Bank's direct loans are made to international buyers and importers to finance purchases of U.S. capital equipment and services and exports to large-sized projects. The bank's direct loan program is what it is best known for. Exports must be shipped from the United States and must have at least 50 percent U.S. content; if less, Ex-Im Bank can only support the U.S. content. Military or defense items are generally not eligible. Also, sales to military buyers are not eligible, with certain exceptions. Exports cannot cause or contribute to adverse economic or environmental effects. Most Ex-Im Bank restrictions on its direct loans are similar to those on its loan guarantees, as discussed below.

Loans typically cover export transactions greater than $10 million; however, Ex-Im Bank points out there are no constraints on the maximum or minimum size of the transaction. The bank's total support is the lower of either 85 percent of the value of all goods and services in the shipment, or 100 percent of the U.S. content. It requires a 15 percent cash down payment. Payback terms are negotiable and are generally longer than seven years.

Working Capital Guarantees

To be eligible for a Working Capital Guarantee, eligible exporters must be located in the United States, must have at least a one-year operating history, and must have a positive net worth. Exports must be shipped from the United States and have at least 50 percent U.S. content; if less, Ex-Im Bank can only support the U.S. content. Military or defense items are generally not eligible. Also, sales to military buyers are not eligible, with certain exceptions.

The financing can be used to purchase finished products for export; pay for raw materials, equipment, supplies, and labor and overhead to produce goods and provide services for export; cover standby letters of credit serving as bid bonds, performance bonds, or payment guarantees; and to finance foreign receivables.

There is no minimum or maximum transaction amount, and up to 90 percent of the loan, including principal and interest, is guaranteed. Loan terms range from one to three years and are secured by export-related receivables and inventory tied to an export order, or 25 percent of the value of letters of credit issued under the guaranteed loan.

Loan Guarantees

Ex-Im Bank typically guarantees loans for importers of U.S. capital equipment and services. Financing may also be available for equipment refurbishing, software, certain banking and legal fees, and certain costs and expenses. Ex-Im Bank notes that there are certain constraints on its guarantees:

- Military or defense items are generally not eligible.

- Sales to military buyers are not eligible, with certain exceptions.
- Goods being exported must meet the bank's foreign content requirements.
- Goods must be shipped from the United States to a foreign buyer.
- U.S. flag vessel requirements must be complied with if the transaction is over $20 million, has repayment terms greater than seven years or the term indicated for a specialized program.

The size of the sale does not affect the buyer's ability to obtain a guarantee although other factors, such as credit ratings, the nature of the buyer, and the transacted goods and services will. The bank's total support is the lesser of 85 percent of the value of all goods and services in the U.S. shipment, or 100 percent of the U.S. content in the U.S. shipment. The guarantee covers 100 percent of principal and interest on any amount, and the bank also offers a medium-term insurance policy for loans up to $10 million. Payback terms up to five years are available for exports of typical capital equipment and services, and terms up to ten years are available for transportation equipment and exports to large-sized projects.

Finance Lease Guarantees

Only finance leases are eligible for bank guarantees. International accounting standards defines a finance lease as "a lease that substantially transfers all the risks and benefits of ownership to the lessee." Ex-Im Bank recognizes that full-payout leases and transactions that work as conditional sales contracts often qualify as finance leases.

In general, only U.S. capital equipment and appurtenant services are eligible for finance lease guarantees, although coverage may also be available for refurbished equipment, software, certain ancillary services (such as banking and legal fees), and certain local costs and services. Military exclusions and exemptions are the same as for Loan Guarantees and Working Capital Guarantees.

City and State Agency Cooperation Program

Ex-Im Bank's City and State Agency Cooperation Program was designed with small, new-to-export companies in mind. The program is intended to simplify access to export assistance by steering new exporters—located in appropriate jurisdictions, of course—toward city, county, state, and other local export finance and development agencies for their loans and guarantees. The bank has forty-four partners located throughout the United States and Puerto Rico.

Many of these local agencies receive funding from the bank and other federal trade-development agencies to produce educational seminars and conferences, as well as to provide technical assistance and guidance to potential exporters.

The Private Export Funding Corporation

The Private Export Funding Corporation (PEFCO) is a private, shareholder organization of several large U.S. banks, multinational corporations, and financial services companies that work very closely with Ex-Im Bank. A partial list of PEFCO's biggest shareholders includes the following:

- J.P. Morgan Chase & Co.
- Bank of America
- ABN AMRO North America
- Citibank, N.A.
- Deutsche Bank (New York)
- Exporters Insurance Corporation
- The Boeing Company
- General Electric Company
- United Technologies Corporation

PEFCO provides financing as a direct lender as well as a secondary market buyer of direct loans originated by other financial institutions. However, these loans must be guaranteed by Ex-Im Bank or, for certain small business export loans, the SBA.

PEFCO is a supplemental lender that can provide financing when many traditional sources choose not to do so. It does this by making the loan and then selling these Ex-Im Bank–guaranteed debts in open markets. The terms of PEFCO's individual long-term direct loans and long-term secured notes require Ex-Im Bank approval.

An exporter may be eligible for PEFCO financing if it meets the following criteria:

- It is a U.S. firm whose lender may be reluctant to finance the exports.
- Its Indian or other non–U.S. buyer is seeking to improve financing terms for their U.S.-sourced imports.
- Its lender qualifies for Ex-Im Bank or SBA support.

U.S. Department of Agriculture (USDA)

Within the U.S. Department of Agriculture, the Foreign Agricultural Service (FAS) has long operated several ongoing programs to assist U.S. farmers to export or compete with foreign imports of agricultural products, such as the following:

- Export guarantee programs that commercially finance agricultural exports
- Dairy Export Incentive Program
- Export Enhancement Program

These programs are administered by the FAS's Office of Trade Programs. Besides these programs, the FAS plays a large role in U.S. trade development and capacity building activities alongside and with other U.S. cabinet-level departments and government agencies. Here's an example of this cooperative vision.

India is the largest agrarian economy on earth, yet many of its people are malnourished—due to inefficient practices and overpopulation—and in need of better farming practices. Also, the Central Government has made agricultural exports a lynchpin in the country's near-term plans to increase exports. The only sustainable way to realize both of these goals is to increase productivity to a Western scale. In 2005, the United States and the Government of India announced the U.S.-India Knowledge Initiative on Agricultural Education, Teaching, Research, Service and Commercial Linkages (AKI) to address the new challenges and opportunities that modern agriculture offers. The AKI is a collaboration of public-private partnerships that offers opportunities for exports of all kinds in the food processing and marketing, biotechnology, water management, and education sectors.

Export-Import Bank of India

You may be asking yourself why I included a foreign export-import bank in a list of options that U.S. exporters should be considering. Well, in my opinion, anything that puts cash in the hands of Indian buyers and importers is good for U.S. exporters. India is furiously financing its own export sector to get badly needed cash into the country. Top Indian experts and policymakers envision manufacturing as their best long-term option to generate those exports, as well as maintain political stability.

The Export-Import Bank of India (Exim Bank) is an Apex financial institution that is wholly owned by the Government of India and managed by representatives of the Central Government, Reserve Bank of India, Export Credit Guarantee Corporation of India, financial institutions, public banks, and the business community. It is organized according to seven operating groups, such as Corporate Banking and Project and Trade Finance. The Lines of Credit group targets small and medium enterprises for assistance. Besides exports, Exim Bank services and finances direct investment, such as the following:

- EOUs for importing technology and services used to develop exports
- Equity participation in Indian exporting companies
- Overseas investments, such as in Latin America, which is close to home for many of us

This bank even finances Bollywood movies! If your Indian customer is clever or well placed, he may be able to leverage Exim Bank's financing and guarantee programs to benefit both of you. Take a few minutes to give the bank's office in Washington, D.C., a call.

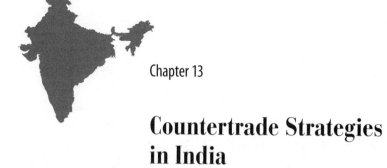

Chapter 13

Countertrade Strategies in India

Exporters always prefer hard cash; however, developing countries like India are generally cash-poor. In order to compete against European and other Asian rivals doing business in India, it is sometimes necessary to negotiate countertrade arrangements specifically suited to a given customer. For those who haven't heard this term yet, countertrade is a contractual arrangement that links exports from one country and imports to another country with limited, or no, use of currency.

Many people have tried to define countertrade in fewer words or more sophisticated economic terms, but it has withstood all these attempts. Barter, offsets, parallel trade, and buybacks are terms used to describe various forms of the same concept, namely, that of handing over something of value (such as exported products) in exchange for something else of value (such as cash, products, or services).

Since the 1950s, countertrade has largely been the domain of military hardware suppliers. Lockheed, Boeing, Grumman, and General Dynamics used countertrade to sell airplanes, guns, and ships to foreign government buyers. Today, the biggest countertraders are Lockheed Martin, Boeing Ventures, British Aerospace, the European ABB Structured Finance division of ABB, and Siemens KFU.

Countertrade in India

Countertrade experts regularly consult with high-level private and Indian government bodies, such as the Confederation of Indian Industries and the Ministry of Defense. Boeing recently sold sixty-eight commercial aircraft (twenty-three Boeing 777s, twenty-seven Boeing 787s, and eighteen Boeing 737s) to Air India (the national, and government-owned, carrier) for delivery through 2011. For the sale price of nearly $8 billion, Boeing agreed to spend over $2 billion of the receipts in unspecified offset countertrade deals.

For many years finance experts attributed 40 to 50 percent of all world trade to some form of countertrade. In 2003, *Foreign Direct Investment* magazine quoted the United Kingdom's minister for international trade, Baroness Symons, as claiming that this ratio was more like 10 to 15 percent of world trade. The Boeing deal falls in between these estimates, which suggests that the estimate of 40 to 50 percent is not unreasonable. It seems, then, that the use of countertrade as a primary marketing tool rather than as a financing technique is becoming more popular every year, especially as constraints on currency convertibility between the United States and India continue to diminish.

India has not published a countertrade policy although the New Delhi government is known to favor its use in defense and civil aviation procurements, the imports of some commodities, and the bulk importation of capital equipment for public-sector infrastructure projects, and encourages private companies to use it when possible. This is made fairly clear by language in global tenders advising bidders that companies willing to use countertrade will be given preference over others. Countertrade deals are reviewed by the Reserve Bank of India and can only be arranged through designated state-owned trading companies, such as the State Trading Corporation for military and essential commodity procurements, and the Mineral and Metals Trading Corporation for civil procurements.

According to the United Kingdom's Trade and Investment information service, imports into India have the following minimum countertrade requirements:

- A 10 to 15 percent counterpurchase ratio for bulk imports of items, such as edible oils and fertilizers valued over 100 million rupees, project-related imports by state-owned companies, purchase of aircraft and aircraft spare parts, and capital imports valued over 1 billion rupees.
- Up to 100 percent counterpurchase ratio for nonessential items such as those used in remanufacture or manufacturing for export, some types of consumer goods, and goods not identified above.
- A 3 percent upfront guarantee of the obligation by the purchaser.

India's Ministry of Commerce has identified goods that state-owned corporations may export under countertrade arrangements. These include agricultural produce, engineering goods, chemical and pharmaceutical products, leather and leather goods, textiles, marine products, and computer software. Most countertrade deals have involved counter purchases by way of imports of goods and services. However, increasing modernization of Indian industry is expected to shift more countertrade deals toward offset trading in the future. On the export side, India's State Trading Corporation also is expected to undertake countertrade obligations in countries against sales of high-value items and technology by Indian companies in collaboration with countertrade exports overseas.

Forms of Countertrade

Those companies who have engaged in countertrade seem to agree that it is not as efficient as the free market, multilateral system. It certainly is complex, risky, and sometimes costly.

Clearly, many exporters, especially smaller companies, will not be able to use countertrade effectively. Nevertheless, those who can use it will find countertrade to be a rational and practical approach to difficult international economic circumstances, such as restrictions on foreign exchange, protectionism, structural limitations, and other external market risks.

Countertrade contracts vary from deal to deal and from customer to customer. Their form and content are limited only by the imagination of the parties involved. Some contracts involve only the exporter and its customer. Others involve third or even fourth parties in other countries. Countertrade contracts may entail payment entirely in goods or services or payment partly in goods and services and partly in cash. The cash portion may be denominated in the currency of the buyer or in that of the exporter. Moreover, a contract may require additional services beyond the mere delivery of goods to be performed either by the exporter or by the buyer. The many variations of countertrade can be discussed under several broad headings:

- Barter
- Compensation
- Parallel trade
- Counterpurchase
- Offsets
- Buybacks
- Co-production

Barter is the oldest form of countertrade and involves exchanging one type of product or service for another. The amount exchanged by each party is determined by negotiation, without invoicing or any exchange of money. To make a barter arrangement work, both parties must either be able to use the goods or sell them at a profit.

Compensation is merely a variation on the barter theme. In this case, the exporter is paid a combination of goods and currency, with the currency denominated either in U.S. dollars or in the buyer's home currency. In the latter case, of course, the exporter must either convert the soft currency to a hard currency or use it in the buyer's country. As with straightforward barter, the exporter must either use the exchanged goods internally or sell them, usually through a countertrade broker.

Parallel trade involves two separate contracts, one for the export sale and one for the purchase of goods from the buyer. Export insurance underwriters as well as trade finance institutions require two contracts so that each side of the transaction may be enforced individually.

Counterpurchase is one of the terms used to describe a parallel trade arrangement involving actual cash transfers. Under such an arrangement, exporter and customer each pay the other for the goods received with drafts, letters of credit, or wire transfers. These payments may be in one currency, or they may be denominated in the home currency of each party. The Indian government is amenable to counterpurchase arrangements as a way to balance imports and exports as well as to stabilize their currency and control inflationary pressures.

Offsets are a more complex form of parallel trade. They may involve a third, or even a fourth, party to the transaction. Exchanged goods then come from a supplier other than the exporter's customer, often from a different country altogether. Most offset transactions involve a corporate seller and a sovereign purchaser, like in the Boeing deal. Products are typically large, high-value items, such as aircraft, military hardware, or infrastructure equipment like turbines, boilers, or smelting furnaces. However, they also may be large orders of high-value goods, such as specialty chemicals. The deal normally involves a package of transactions carried out over a defined period of time and theoretically compensates the importing country for loss of jobs, currency exchange, and the development of similar technologies within the buyer's country. Here is how an offset transaction might be structured:

1. Your company owns a manufacturing plant in Thailand that produces mining equipment components you then assemble in the United States.
2. You want to sell mining equipment to the Indian government, which doesn't have enough hard currency to pay for it.
3. Your company agrees to finance the building of a state-owned cement plant in India in exchange for a 40 percent equity interest.
4. Your company secures the balance of the necessary financing for the cement plant from USAID.
5. Cement made in this new plant is exported to Thailand and paid for with Thai baht, which are then used by the Indian government to pay you for the mining equipment.
6. Your company uses the baht to pay operating expenses in the Thai plant.

Everyone wins in this kind of deal. The Indian government creates jobs, foreign exchange, and a viable industry. As the cement business grows, you should be able to reap profits from your 40 percent equity ownership. Also, of course, you succeed in closing the original export order.

Buyback arrangements are quite common for the sale of technology, licenses, production lines, or even complete factories. Many U.S. companies use buybacks to import subassemblies, components, or parts needed for the completion of finished products. Buyback products also could be sold on the open market. Buybacks are especially popular for turnkey projects such as factories, warehouses, resorts, hospitals, or infrastructure facilities. Here is an example of how a turnkey buyback transaction might be structured:

1. The customer first pays for the project with government-backed long-term credit.
2. The exporter then agrees either to buy back products or services from the completed facility or to serve as a distributor for products exported from the host country.
3. The host-country customer uses these hard currency payments to liquidate the original long-term credit.

In a variation on this scheme, no cash changes hands, and no credit arrangements are necessary. The countertrade contract merely states that the output from the newly constructed facility will be applied to the original price of the exports. However, with this type of arrangement, you should insist on a bank guarantee to ensure that the contracted output from the new facility will be produced and shipped on schedule.

Co-production is a specialized form of buyback countertrade used principally for the transfer of technology or management expertise. The following example describes a typical co-production arrangement:

1. Assume that you want to sell desktop printers in India.
2. An Indian company wants to purchase the printers but also wants the technology to produce them at home.
3. Your two companies form a joint venture to build a suburban Mumbai plant to manufacture the printers.
4. Your company takes an equity interest in the project and may also furnish management support to run the facility. In either case, the facility is usually co-constructed by exporter and customer.

As both parties remain responsible for the operation of the facility, manufacturing the printers is known as co-production. The benefits of such an arrangement are the following:

1. With equity interests, both parties profit from printer sales.
2. The Indian customer gains new technology.
3. Most important, you have made an export sale.

To avoid any misunderstanding, let's clarify one point. The terms used in countertrade—compensation, counter-purchase, co-production, and so on—are not essential to the structuring of a countertrade deal. You can call the deal anything you want and structure it any way you want as long as it benefits both you and your customer.

Countertrade Guidelines

Developing a trade finance strategy is never easy. Many alternatives must be considered, including the long-term benefits and risks of countertrade arrangements. Because of financial, contractual, and administrative complexities, countertrade should only be used when more conventional financing is not practical. Although certainly not all-inclusive, the following guidelines offer a good starting point for minimizing countertrade risks:

1. Establish a risk threshold that is measurable in terms of money expended, time required, and administrative difficulty. Beyond this threshold, the transaction will become uneconomical and should be terminated.
2. Identify a countertrade broker capable of selling exchanged goods.
3. Insist on adequate shipping and collection insurance as well as on bank guarantees of customer performance.
4. Get a clear interpretation of the terms of the counter-trade contract from a competent professional.
5. Structure the deal as simply as possible to reduce the risk of an unmanageable contract.

Finally, be aware that every countertrade deal stands alone, with features unique to that transaction. There is no set formula you can apply. There are no regulations you must follow. And, with a few minor exceptions, governments will not interfere with the details of the transaction as long as the economic and political policies of the host country are not violated.

For more information on how countertrade might fit into your marketing plans, contact the U.S. Trade Association, Global Offset and Countertrade Association, 818 Connecticut Avenue, NW, 12th Floor, Washington, D.C. 20006. Also, the supposedly defunct Asia Pacific Countertrade Association still maintains a Web site (*www.apca.net*), presumably as a portal for its principals to solicit consulting business. Furthermore, the Web site's claim that its Conference Series is now a collaborative effort with the United Nations Conference on Trade and Development (UNCTAD) suggests that countertrade is alive and doing well throughout Asia.

U.S. Government

Bureau of Economic Analysis (U.S. Department of Commerce)
www.bea.gov

Bureau of Industry and Security (U.S. Department of Commerce)
www.bis.doc.gov

Bureau of Public Affairs (U.S. State Department)
www.state.gov/r/pa

CIA World Factbook, India (U.S. Central Intelligence Agency)
https://www.cia.gov/cia/publications/factbook/geos/in.html

Commercial Service (U.S. Department of Commerce)
www.buyusa.gov

U.S. Department of Commerce
www.commerce.gov

U.S. Economic Development Administration
www.eda.gov

U.S. Economics and Statistics Administration
www.esa.doc.gov

Embassy of the United States, New Delhi, India
http://newdelhi.usembassy.gov

Export Assistance Centers (U.S. Small Business Administration)
www.sba.gov/oit/export/useac.html

Export.gov (U.S. Commercial Service)
www.export.gov

Export-Import Bank of the United States
www.exim.gov

Foreign Agricultural Service (U.S. Department of Agriculture)
www.fas.usda.gov

International Catalog Exhibition Program (U.S. Department of Commerce)
www.export.gov/comm_svc/catalog_program.html

International Company Profiles (U.S. Department of Commerce)
www.export.gov/comm_svc/intl_co_profile.html

International Trade Administration (U.S. Department of Commerce)
www.trade.gov

Market Access and Compliance Office (U.S. Department of Commerce)
www.trade.gov/mac

Minority Business Development Agency (U.S. Department of Commerce)
www.mbda.gov
National Institute of Standards and Technology (U.S. Department of Commerce)
www.nist.gov
Office of Technology Policy (U.S. Department of Commerce)
www.technology.gov/otpolicy
Office of Small and Disadvantaged Business Utilization Minority Resource Center
www.usaid.gov/business/small_business
Offices of Manufacturing and Services (U.S. Department of Commerce)
www.trade.gov/mas
Overseas Private Investment Corporation
www.opic.gov
Patent and Trademark Office (U.S. Department of Commerce)
www.uspto.gov
U.S. Small Business Administration
www.sba.gov
Technology Administration (U.S. Department of Commerce)
www.technology.gov
U.S. Trade and Development Agency
www.tda.gov
Trade Compliance Center (U.S. Department of Commerce)
http://ttc.export.gov
U.S. Agency for International Development
www.usaid.gov

Republic of India Government

Census of India
www.censusindia.net
Central Statistical Organization (Ministry of Statistics and Programme Implementation)
www.mospi.nic.in/cso_test1.htm
Department of Industrial Policy and Promotion
www.dipp.nic.in
Department of Secondary and Higher Education (Ministry of Human Resource Development)
www.education.nic.in/adledu.asp
Embassy of India, Washington, D.C.
www.indianembassy.org
Export-Import Bank of India
www.eximbankindia.com

Government of India Directory
www.goidirectory.nic.in
India in Business (sponsored by the Ministry of External Affairs)
www.indiainbusiness.nic.in
India Vision 2020
www.india2020.org.in
Ministry of Corporate Affairs
www.mca.gov.in
Ministry of Finance
www.finmin.nic.in
National Informatics Centre—Patents (Department of Information Technology)
http://patinfo.nic.in/
National Portal of the Government of India
www.india.gov.in
Planning Commission
www.planningcommission.nic.in
Press Information Bureau
www.pib.nic.in
Reserve Bank of India
www.rbi.org.in/home.aspx
Tenders Information System
www.tenders.gov.in/index.htm

International Agencies

Asian Development Bank
www.adb.org
International Finance Corporation
www.ifc.org
International Monetary Fund
www.imf.org
Multilateral Investment Guarantee Agency
www.miga.org
Organization for Economic Cooperation and Development
www.oecd.org
The World Bank
www.worldbank.org
United Nations Conference on Trade and Development
www.unctad.org

United Nations Development Program
www.undp.org
United Nations Educational, Scientific, and Cultural Organization
www.unesco.org
World Trade Organization
www.wto.org

Private-Sector Organizations
U.S. Organizations

American Association of Exporters and Importers
www.aaei.org
Confederation of Indian Industry
www.ciionline.org
Federation of International Trade Associations
www.fita.org/countries/indiaportal.html
Foreign Credit Insurance Association
www.fcia.com
National Customs Brokers and Forwarders Association of America, Inc.
www.ncbfaa.org
National Foreign Trade Council
www.nftc.org
Private Export Funding Corporation (PEFCO)
www.pefco.com/index.htm
Small Business Exporters Association
www.sbea.org
U.S.-India Business Council
www.usibc.com

Indian Organizations

American Chamber of Commerce in India
www.amchamindia.com
Indian Banks' Association
www.iba.org.in
Federation of Indian Chambers of Commerce and Industry (FICCI)
www.ficci.com
Franchising Association of India
www.fai.co.in/test/index.php3
India Direct Marketing Association
www.direct-marketing-association-india.org

Other Resources and Web Sites
Businesses and Organizations

Corporation for International Business
www.atacarnet.com

CRISIL (business & credit ratings firm owned by Standard & Poor's)
www.crisil.com

eLease International, Inc.
www.eleaseinternational.com

Global Offset and Countertrade Association
www.globaloffset.org

International Company Profile
www.icpcredit.com

International Factors Group
www.ifgroup.com

International Forfaiting Association
www.forfaiters.org

InternetLC.com
www.internetlc.com

Lease Force International
www.leaseforce.com

World Economic Forum
www.weforum.org

World Trade Centers Association
http://world.wtca.org

News and Media

Business Standard
www.business-standard.com
Hindu Business Line
www.thehindubusinessline.com
Rediff—India Abroad
www.rediff.com
The Economic Times
www.economictimes.indiatimes.com
The Financial Express
www.financialexpress.com
The Times of India
www.timesofindia.indiatimes.com

The U.S. Department of Commerce suggests the following as being the leading business sectors for U.S. involvement. Several of these products are listed in mature U.S. trade agreements with India. Like everything else in India, this list is likely to change as new avenues open and business sectors develop.

Agricultural Sectors
- Cotton
- Tree nuts and dry fruit (excluding cashews)
- Wood products
- Fresh fruits and pulses
- Vegetable oil

Commercial and Financial Sectors
- Airport and ground-handling equipment
- Banking
- Broadcasting
- Computers and peripheral equipment
- Education services
- Electric power (generation, distribution, and transmission equipment)
- Food-processing equipment
- Health care
- Infrastructure (such as roads, ports)
- Insurance
- Machine tools
- Medical equipment
- Mining and mineral-processing equipment (such as for coal)
- Oil-field and gas-field machinery
- Pension fund management
- Petroleum refining and petrochemical manufacturing
- Pharmaceuticals (research, development, manufacturing)
- Pollution-control equipment
- Process-control equipment
- Safety-and-security equipment
- Software services
- Telecommunications equipment
- Water (wells, pumps, purification, and wastewater treatment)

Index